Local Public Finance and the Fiscal Squeeze: A Case Study

Local Public Finance and the Fiscal Squeeze: A Case Study

Edited by
John R. Meyer and
John M. Quigley

with contributions by
Christopher H. Gadsden
Malcolm Getz
Peter Kemper
Robert A. Leone
Roger W. Schmenner

Ballinger Publishing Company ● Cambridge, Massachusetts
A Subsidiary of J.B. Lippincott Company

International Standard Book Number: 0-88410-287-4

Library of Congress Catalog Card Number: 76-15619

Printed in the United States of America

Library of Congress Cataloging in Publication Data

Main entry under title:

Local public finance and the fiscal squeeze.

Papers from a seminar sponsored by the Institution for Social and Policy Studies at Yale University and the Yale Law School, held during the academic years 1971-72 and 1972-73.
Includes bibliographical references.
1. Finance, Public—New Haven—Congresses. 2. Taxation—New Haven—Congresses. 3. Municipal services—Connecticut—New Haven—Finance—Congresses. I. Meyer, John Robert. II. Quigley, John Michael. III. Yale University. Institution for Social and Policy Studies. IV. Yale University. School of Law.

Library of Congress Cataloging in Publication Data
HJ9211.N4L63   336   76-15619
ISBN 0-88410-287-4

Contents

List of Figures   ix

List of Tables   xi

Acknowledgments   xv

Chapter One
Fiscal Influences Upon Location Patterns
John R. Meyer and *John M. Quigley*   1

Expanding the Tax Base   19

Chapter Two
Prospects for Economic Development:
The New Haven Case
Malcolm Getz and *Robert A. Leone*   21

The Nature of Economic Development   21
The Development Issues for New Haven   22
Economic Change and Development Prospects
    in New Haven   25
Change in the Manufacturing Sector   25
Change in Individual Industries   27
Nonmanufacturing Employment   31
A Perspective on Relocating Plants   35
Summary Observations   38

Chapter Three
Tax Exemption and the Local Property Tax
Robert A. Leone and *John R. Meyer*   41

The Budgetary Impact of Tax-Exempt Properties on Host
Municipalities: A Case Study of Yale and New Haven   41
Summary and Conclusions   51
Appendix: The Calculations of Direct Costs   55
Fire   56
Police   58
Sewerage   60
Streets   62
Lights   64
Parks and Recreation   64
Allocating Services to Yale University   66

Chapter Four
Municipal Income Taxation
Christopher H. Gadsden and *Roger W. Schmenner*   69

I—Brief History of the Municipal Income Tax   69
II—Describing the Property and Municipal Income Taxes   70
Double Taxation   71
Apportioning Business Income Subject to Tax   72
Other Issues   73
Diversity in the Municipal Income Tax   73
III—Evaluating the Property and Income Taxes   74
Tax Incidence   74
Vertical Equity   77
Horizontal Equity   78
Economic Efficiency and Location Incentives   79
Administrative Cost   80
Summary   81
IV—Legal Authority to Tax Income   81
Threshold Barriers   81
Legal Constraints on the Type of Income Tax   82
  Tax Base   82
  Wages and Salaries   83
  Rents, Dividends, and Capital Gains   84
  Corporate and Unincorporated Business Association Income   85
  Rate Structure   85
V—Municipal Income Taxation: Variations and Alternatives   87
Inter-municipal Cooperation   87
The Metropolitan Taxing District   88

State-Local Cooperation   88
Federal-Local or Federal-State-Local Cooperation   89
VI—Municipal Income Taxation and the New Haven Area   90
Tax Bill Estimates by Type of Property   92
Tax Burdens Under Various Incidence Assumptions   95

Efficiency in Service Provision   99

Chapter Five
Refuse Collection Policy
Peter Kemper and *John M. Quigley*   01

Financing by User Charges   102
Collection Costs   110
The Need for Government Intervention   118

Chapter Six
Fire Fighting Benefits
Malcolm Getz and *Robert A. Leone*   121

Fire Services in New Haven   122
Fire Expenditures, Losses, and Insurance Ratings
    in Connecticut Towns   133
Summary   140

Chapter Seven
Police Services—Their Costs and Financing
Peter Kemper and *Roger W. Schmenner*   143

The Cost of Police Services   144
The Nature of Police Services   144
From a Line Item to a Program Budget   146
Results   153
Financing Police Services by Special Charges   157
The Efficiency of Special Charges   157
The Distributional Impact of Police Services   162
Assessment of Special Charges   169
Summary   170
Appendix A   173
Appendix B   181
Appendix C   183
Appendix D   185

Chapter Eight
Findings and Implications
John R. Meyer and *John M. Quigley*   187

Notes   195

About the Editors   203

List of Figures

5-1   Average Collection Time Versus Density
for New Haven Sample   115

7-1   Procedure for Estimating Costs for Individual
Police Services   147

7-2   Crime Grids, Bridgeport, Connecticut   154

7-3   Nominal Incidence of Property Tax and
Total Expenditures   169

List of Tables

1-1   Sources of Local Government Revenue   6
1-2   Distribution of Local Government Expenditures,
        1972, as Percent of Total Expenditure   8
1-3   Concentration of Low Income Households
        in Central Cities for Selected SMSAs, 1950,
        1960, 1970   10
1-4   Average Effective Property Tax Rates in
        Central City and Suburban Parts of
        Metropolitan Areas   11
1-5   Comparisons of Tax Exempt Real Property
        in Central Cities and Their Suburban Rings   14
1-6   Concentration of Transportation, Communica-
        tion, and Utility Workers in Central City and
        Suburban Locations   16
1-7   Ratio of Median to Mean Income, for Selected
        Metropolitan Areas, 1970   16
2-1   New Haven SMSA Manufacturing Establish-
        ments: Movers, Non-movers, Births, and Deaths,
        by Municipality 1967-1971   26
2-2   Origins and Destinations of Manufacturing
        Relocations, 1967-1971   28
2-3   Births in Manufacturing Industries, New Haven
        SMSA, 1967-1971   29
2-4   Movers in Manufacturing Industries, New Haven
        SMSA, 1967-1971, by Industry and
        Establishment Size   32

2–5	Births and Movers in Nonmanufacturing Industries, New Haven SMSA, 1967–1971, 20 and Over Employees	34
3–1	Tax-Exempt Property in New Haven, 1970	43
3–2	Direct Services to the Tax-Exempt Property of Yale University, by Property Class, and Yale's Hypothetical Tax Bill, 1971–1972	49
3–3	Net Costs to the University for Public Service Programs, 1971	50
3A–1	Firefighting Budget	56
3A–2	Fire-Vulnerable Property, by Land Use, 1970	57
3A–3	Summary Information for Three Universities Supplying Their Own Fire Protection	58
3A–4	Allocation of Police Expenses	59
3A–5	Distribution of Police Expenses, by Property Class	60
3A–6	Allocation of Sewerage Expenses to Property Type	63
3A–7	Cost of Sewerage System	63
3A–8	Percent of Total Time Spent on Street Maintenance Activities, by Property Use	65
3A–9	Percentage of Total Value of Street Lighting Services Attributable to Property Type	65
3A–10	Total Operating Budget for Parks and Recreational Services, Allocable and Nonallocable	65
3A–11	Final Allocation of Total Budget for Parks and Recreational Services	67
3A–12	Breakdown of Yale Property (In Terms of Assessed Value) According to Land Use	67
3A–13	Assignment of Public Services Allocated to Yale, by Property Type	67
4–1	Comparative Table of Local Income Taxes in Ten Major Cities as of 7/1/73	75
4–2	Wages as Percent of Adjusted Gross Income, by Income Class, North Atlantic Region	78
4–3	New Haven Income Tax Base Estimates—1970	93
4–4	New Haven Area Commutation Patterns	94
4–5	Short Run New Haven Tax Burdens—Municipal Income Tax Completely Replaces Property Tax	95
4–6	Short Run New Haven Tax Burdens—$10 Million (¼ of $40 Million) Raised by Service-Related Property Tax and $30 Million Raised by Income Tax	96
4–7	Short Run New Haven Tax Burdens—Property and Income Taxes Levied at Same Rate on Income and Property Services Flows	97

5-1	Refuse Generation and Incidence of User Charges for Refuse Collection	106
5-2	Estimated Tax Saving Due to Federal Deductibility of Local Taxes	108
5-3	Estimates of Refuse Collection Costs per Minute for New Haven in 1972	116
6-1	Fire-by-Fire Loss Analysis	124
6-2	Fire-by-Fire Loss Analysis—Fire Damage Equation (Working Fires Only)	125
6-3	Fire-by-Fire Loss Analysis—Casualty Equation (Working Fires Only)	126
6-4	Benefit Calculations with Counterfactual Assumption I, New Haven 1968–1972—Benefits to Property Assuming Total Structure Loss for Every Fire	129
6-5	Benefit Calculations with Counterfactual Assumption II, New Haven 1968–1972—Benefits to Property Assuming Total Structure Loss for Every Fire	130
6-6	Benefit Calculations with Counterfactual Assumption III, New Haven 1968–1972—Benefits to Property Adjusted for Out-on-Arrival Fires, Structure Characteristics and Fire Units	132
6-7	Benefit Calculations with Counterfactual Assumption IV, New Haven 1968–1972— Benefits to Life Not Adjusted for Out-on-Arrival	134
6-8	Fire Expenditures, Losses and Insurance Ratings—List of Variables for Three-Equation Models	138
6-9	Fire Loss and Expenditure in Connecticut Town	139
7-1	Manpower Chart of the Bridgeport Police Department	145
7-2	Police Costs, by Type of Expense, 1972–1973	149
7-3	Capital Equipment	150
7-4	Costs by Division, 1972–1973	151
7-5	Degree of Detective Followup, by Type of Incident	155
7-6	Police Costs, by Type of Service, 1973	156
7-7	Police Expenses, by Type of Service	164
7-8	Comparison of the Nominal Incidence of Expenditures and Property Taxes	165
7-9	Nominal Incidence Regressions for Property Taxes and Police Expenditures for City Residents	168

7A–1   Private Allocation of Patrol and Detective
        Division Costs   174
7A–2   Auto Allocation of Patrol and Detective
        Division Costs   175
7A–3   City-wide Allocation of Patrol and Detective
        Division Costs   176
7A–4   Residential Allocation of Patrol and Detective
        Division Costs   177
7A–5   Commercial-Industrial Allocation of Patrol
        and Detective Division Costs   178
7B–1   Mean Times per Incident for High Incidence
        Calls for Service, by Section of the City   181
7C–1   Mean Times per Incident, by General Category
        of Call, for Broadly Defined Sections of City   183
7D–1   Spatial Variation in Annual Neighborhood
        Service Costs   186

Acknowledgments

During the academic years 1971–72 and 1972–73 the Institution for Social and Policy Studies at Yale University and the Yale Law School jointly sponsored a seminar on the regional economy and the problems facing the local public sector. Besides students and faculty from Yale University, the seminar included several representatives of other universities, of the local business community, and of local government. During 1971–1972, the seminar was organized by John R. Meyer and John G. Simon; in 1972–1973 it was organized by John M. Quigley and Roger W. Schmenner.

The chapters in this volume were prepared for this joint seminar, and the authors acknowledge the assistance of their numerous colleagues in this enterprise. We also acknowledge the intellectual and financial support of the Institution for Social and Policy Studies and of its Directors, John Perry Miller and Charles E. Lindblom. Additional financial support was provided by the National Science Foundation under grant number GI 39589. We are particularly indebted to Robert Goldman of NSF for his encouragement of this research. We also acknowledge the dedicated research assistance of Debra Stinson, Gail Trask, and Johanna Zimmer-Hart, and the expert typing of Janice Clancey and Diane Slider.

In addition to the papers reported in this volume, several related analyses are available.

From the Institution for Social and Policy Studies, Yale University:

Henry B. Hansmann, "User Charges and the Law," 43 pp.

Charles J. Stokes, "New Haven 1870–1970: Growth and Transformation of an American Industrial Center," 45 pp.

A. Tappan Wilder, "Reach and Grasp: Perspective on New Haven's First Three Hundred Years," 22 pp.

From Ballinger Publishing Co.:

Richard J. Murnane, *The Impact of School Resources on the Learning of Inner City Children*, 125 pp.

Peter Kemper and John M. Quigley, *The Economics of Refuse Collection*, 200 pp.

John M. Quigley
New Haven

Local Public Finance and the Fiscal Squeeze: A Case Study

※ *Chapter 1*

Fiscal Influences Upon Location Patterns

John R. Meyer
John M. Quigley

Economic analyses of the urban spatial structure emphasize the importance of changes in transportation costs, technology, personal income, and external economies on patterns of locational change for firms and households. These analyses traditionally describe the locational choices of firms in terms of the transport cost of factor inputs (labor force assembly and materials), the costs of actual production, and the costs of delivering goods to markets.[1] Accordingly, two key factors are usually singled out as particularly responsible for the central concentrations of industrial and commercial activity in urban areas. First, for a wide variety of activities, central locations generally minimize the sum of transport costs—i.e., the costs of assembling physical inputs and labor and the costs of distributing final products. Second, and largely independent of transport costs, the physical proximity of large numbers of firms results in significant production savings for a wide variety of activities. These "agglomeration economies," or external economies of scale, may result from any of several influences, including complementarity in the supply of labor, materials, business services, and information.

For households, the traditional economic approach emphasizes the importance of the costs of commutation to a central employment location in motivating location choices;[2] that is, households' residential locations are seen as being determined by the trade-off between the costs of commuting an additional distance to the city center and the savings arising from cheaper land or housing services at greater distances from the center. Under normal assumptions, this logic implies that higher income households consume more space

1

than lower income households, that they commute longer distances to the city center, and that housing prices and residential densities decline with distance to the center.[3]

These economic analyses of the determinants of urban spatial structure yield important insights about the factors responsible for the initial growth of American cities and for the general structure of land use in many large urban areas. Nevertheless, the factors emphasized in these models have become substantially less relevant to an understanding of the marginal adjustments of land use patterns which have been made over the last half-century in virtually all American cities. Moreover, the relevance of these traditional theories to land use changes in smaller metropolitan areas, where absolute transport cost differentials have always been smaller in magnitude, is particularly questionable.

Several developments suggest a reduced importance for transport cost differentials as an explanation of the urban spatial structure. Above all, the technical characteristics of transport and communication have changed markedly. Historically, there were powerful market forces attracting both firms producing output for local consumption and firms producing output for "export" to the core of metropolitan areas. Before the introduction of the truck and the development of the interstate highway system, firms that relied upon "imports" of raw materials, or that "exported" output, were tied to central distribution facilities, typically ports or railroad yards at central locations.

During the second decade of the century, the truck was introduced for intraregional shipment, reducing this attraction towards the central core, especially for firms producing locally consumed output.[4] However, firms that relied upon "imported" raw materials or which "exported" goods to national markets were still tied to central locations with access to rail or port facilities. The development of the system of interstate motor transport, beginning in the 1920s, substantially weakened this linkage. With the development of a national highway network, it became possible for firms to choose locations remote from the historical concentration of industrial activity at the central business district at little cost in terms of accessibility.

Parallel developments in the fields of communications, information flow, and data processing reduced the spatial importance of agglomeration economies during the same period. Communication by telephone, electronic data processing, and related advances reduced the importance of physical proximity in exploiting external economies of scale. While these external economies remained as important as ever, they could now be fully exploited by most firms in a metropolitan area without geographic proximity. Thus both of the sufficient conditions for the centralization of firm locations in metropolitan areas have become less binding over the past several decades. Land suitable for commercial and industrial use has become available at far more sites, or equivalently, central and noncentral sites have become far more homogeneous. In short, the relative advantage of any particular site, measured by its transport or agglomerative characteristics, has declined.

In fact, other technical changes in production may have increased the absolute advantage of noncentral sites, at least for many types of industrial production. For many, if not most industrial processes, technical change has reduced the relative cost of high land-to-capital ratios in production. The continuous flow processes, which have increasingly characterized "best practice" technology not only in such large scale activities as iron and steel production and aluminum refining but also smaller scale activities such as baking and brewing, have increased the relative advantage of single-story plants in a wide variety of production processes. The prohibitive cost of converting high density downtown building configurations to accommodate this "best practice" technology has made vacant land, which is ubiquitous at suburban locations but virtually nonexistent at central locations, increasingly attractive for the location of industrial activity.

In the light of these trends in industrial locations, the analysis of households' residential location needs reorientation. Even if it is assumed that households' choices of residential location result from the systematic substitution of journey-to-work costs for housing costs, it is less and less true that these costs are measured by access to the center of any urban area. In particular, the increasing suburbanization of households results not merely from rising incomes and transport improvements, but from the peripheral or suburban locations of households' work sites.

If this view is correct, it has important consequences for economic analysis of determinants of residential and industrial location and of the changes in the spatial structure of most urban areas. If transport costs to the urban core and agglomerative economies are less important in motivating the site choice of firms, and as a result are less important in motivating the site choices of households, the question naturally arises: have other site specific variations in the costs of alternative locations decreased as well? If the answer to this question is affirmative, it suggests that economic considerations are less important generally in intrametropolitan location decisions.

In addition to transport and external economies, there are probably two other sources of site specific variation in firm costs. The first—labor force assembly costs—has become less site specific during the same period, if only because of the increased importance of commutation by private auto relative to radial public transit. In fact, for certain types of specialized industrial and commercial activity (for example, research and development activities and headquarters activities for multiestablishment firms) suburban locations may be more accessible to the residences of potential workers. A similar advantage may exist for activities employing secondary wage earners, particularly clerical and other white collar personnel.

The second source of site specific variation in location costs for firms and households includes the taxes paid and public services received at alternative locations. In contrast to all the other costs associated with alternative location decisions, there are strong reasons to believe that the intraregional variation in taxes and in public services has increased substantially during the past several decades. Several factors appear to be responsible for this. First and most obviously, with improvements in transport and with the increasing geographic size of metropolitan areas, the geographic size of an identifiable labor market or a market for local output has increased substantially. Yet the number of political jurisdictions in the United States as a whole has remained relatively stable over the past 40 or 50 years. Thus, the number of jurisdictions accessible within, say, a half-hour commute of any central city has increased several fold. In principle, each of these jurisdictions could provide a different set of tax levies and a different package of local services.

Beyond the increasing number of accessible jurisdictions, the resources devoted to local public output have increased substantially, and the relative costs of public services have risen appreciably. For example, per capita spending by state and local governments has increased in real terms by 305 percent during the period 1945–1967. Measured as a share of gross national product, state and local expenditures have increased from 5 percent of GNP to 12 percent during the same period.[5] In part, these increases have resulted from the presumably high income elasticity of demand for public services (e.g., education), but they also have reflected rising input prices in labor intensive activities. Crude estimates have indicated that when the quantities of inputs have been held constant, unit costs of local output have risen at a compound rate of 5 to 7 percent during the postwar period, or at a rate of four to five times as fast as the index of wholesale prices.[6]

There is little reason to expect reversal in these trends. Education, police and fire protection, and refuse collection, for example, are highly labor intensive activities—activities in which the technical possibilities of substituting capital for labor are sharply limited, at least when compared to manufacturing or agriculture. If labor productivity, both average and marginal, is substantially lower in the service sector, and if rough wage parity is maintained between the manufacturing and service sectors of the economy, this implies that the costs of maintaining a given level of public output will continue to rise over time. In response to these increases in costs and the corresponding increases in the tax rates required to finance them, we may expect different reactions in local jurisdictions; these will range from curtailment of services, to the pursuit of more efficient methods of service delivery, to the introduction of alternative financing instruments, depending upon the price and income elasticities of demands by the voters and the perceptions and abilities of local officials.

The influence of the public sector upon the location decisions of firms and households is further strengthened by the particular nature of the taxes and the services available at alternative locations. On the revenue side, the local property tax is, and historically has been, the dominant source of local funds. As Table 1-1 indicates, for all local governments, receipts from property taxation amounted to almost two-thirds of all locally raised revenues in 1972, and were about five times as important, in terms of local revenue, as all other local tax sources combined. When intergovernmental transfers are included, receipts from local property taxes still accounted for almost 40 percent of the general revenues of local governments.

As shown in Table 1-1, the reliance upon other forms of taxation increased only modestly over the past two decades. As a percent of locally raised revenue, receipts from sales and gross receipts taxes and from personal income taxes increased from 3 percent in 1942 to 10 percent in 1972. Nevertheless, locally assessed levies on real property are still the cornerstone of local finance. Table 1-1 also presents comparable information for a single city, New Haven, which will be analyzed in some detail in this monograph. As compared with the data for local governments as a whole, the table indicates that property taxation is even more important as a source of revenue in this city. Levies against real property currently account for more than 90 percent of locally raised revenues, and there is little trend toward increased reliance upon other forms of taxation.

Historically, the primary reason for singling out property as an object of taxation has been the ostensible immobility of land. Although land itself may be immobile, the above analysis strongly suggests that the functions performed on urban land have become

Table 1-1. Sources of Local Government Revenue

Sources of Revenue	*Percent of General Revenue from Local Sources*				*Percent of General Revenue*			
	1942	*1957*	*1967*	*1972*	*1942*	*1957*	*1967*	*1972*
All Local Governments								
General revenue from local sources	100.0	100.0	100.0	100.0	74.0	70.0	65.3	62.3
Property taxes	80.8	69.3	66.2	63.5	60.0	48.7	43.2	39.6
Sales & gross receipts	2.5	5.8	5.1	6.5	1.9	4.1	3.4	4.1
Personal income tax	0.5	1.1	2.4	3.4	0.4	0.8	1.6	2.1
Corporate income tax	0.1	–	–	–	–	–	–	–
Other taxes	3.6	3.8	2.7	2.5	2.7	2.7	1.7	1.5
Current charges	12.5	20.0	16.5	16.9	9.3	14.1	10.8	10.5
Miscellaneous			7.1	7.2			4.5	4.5
Intergovernmental revenue					26.0	29.7	34.7	37.7
New Haven								
General revenue from local sources	100.0	100.0	100.0	100.0	95.6	86.7	85.8	80.9
Property taxes	85.2	95.2	88.2	91.6	81.4	82.5	75.7	74.2
Sales & gross receipts	1.0	–	1.3	2.5	1.0	–	1.1	2.0
Personal income tax	–	–	–	–	–	–	–	–
Corporate income tax	–	–	–	–	–	–	–	–
Other taxes	7.2	0.7	0.6	0.6	6.9	0.6	0.5	0.5
Current charges	1.1	2.4	1.7	2.5	1.1	2.1	1.5	2.0
Miscellaneous	5.5	1.8	8.2	2.8	5.2	1.5	7.0	2.2
Intergovernmental revenue					4.4	13.4	14.2	19.1

Source:
U.S. Bureau of the Census, *Census of Governments*, U.S. Government Printing Office: 1957, Vol. 3, No. 5; 1962, Vol. 4, No. 4; 1967, Vol. 4, No. 5; 1972, Vol. 4, No. 5.
City of New Haven, *Budget, City of New Haven, Connecticut*, 1943, 1959, 1969, 1974.

increasingly mobile during the past half-century. Moreover, the potential for mobility in response to excise levies on real property has increased as the number of proximate jurisdictions with similar parcels has increased. The mobility of the occupants of land parcels is indeed high in the United States. For example, it appears that about 20 percent of American households relocate annually, and more than two-thirds of these relocations are short distance moves within a single urban area.[7] Other evidence suggests that the physical location of as much as 10 percent of the jobs in an urban area changes each year.[8] Many of these household relocations may be "caused" by demographic factors (that is, by changes in family size and composition), or by changes in job location. Similarly, many of these employment relocations may be caused by changes in market demands, resulting in "births" and "deaths" of individual establishments and the expansion or contraction of employment at particular sites.

Regardless of the proximate cause of decisions to change the spatial location for housing consumption or business activity, economic theory suggests that both firms and households engaged in relocation will employ some cost minimizing strategy in evaluating alternative destinations. For example, even though a firm's decision to relocate in a given year may be caused by increases in the demand for its output that cannot be accommodated at its current location, its choice among alternative sites in the metropolitan area should be heavily responsive to cost differentials—those composed of aggregate transport costs, agglomerative considerations, and tax and public service variations.

With regard to the spatial variations in public outputs, it should be noted that the proceeds of local excise levies are typically used to finance three conceptually distinct types of local activities. First, some component of the property tax represents a flat or highly averaged "service charge" for certain publicly provided services to real property, services which to a greater or a lesser extent can be rendered by private property owners themselves or by voluntary associations of such property owners. Perhaps the most concrete examples are such services as refuse removal, street lighting and maintenance, and sewerage, which are provided as local "public" services in some communities, but which are left to the private sector in others.

Similarly, many police and fire protection services are often rendered as private goods. For example, in different communities, activities such as emergency ambulance service and traffic control at private parking lots are as easily identified with the private sector as with the public sector. The total of such highly averaged service charges as a proportion of local expenditures is not insignificant.

The local property tax is also composed of substantial levies designed to support "true" public goods (in the narrow economists' sense) and income redistribution programs. Examples of pure public goods may include the local courts and many public health activities. Locally financed welfare programs may also have public good characteristics, but they are typically designed with income distribution objectives in mind.

By far the largest single component of the public good–redistribution activities supported by the local government budget is public education, which typically accounts for the largest fraction of local public outlays. Table 1-2 shows the distribution of governmental expenditures in 1972 for all local governments and, for comparison, for New Haven as well. The table indicates that education accounts for over 40 percent of local outlays. Public health and welfare expenditures, primarily redistributive in nature, account for another 13 percent of outlays. Police, fire, sanitation, parks, roads, and utilities—a substantial portion of which provide private benefits to particular residents and property owners—comprise almost 30 percent of local expenditures.

Obviously, the classification of a particular activity as being a private good supplied to property users, and thus not a part of the excise component of the local property tax, is somewhat ambiguous. Nevertheless, the conceptual distinction is clear. This distinction is, moreover, extremely useful in analyzing the location choices of firms

Table 1-2. Distribution of Local Government Expenditures, 1972, as Percent of Total Expenditure[1]

Function	All Local Governments	New Haven City
Education	41.24	35.6
Highways & transportation	6.59	2.6
Hospitals, public welfare & health	13.47	5.4
Police, fire & correction	7.20	14.5
Sewerage & sanitation	4.10	15.8
Parks, recreation & natural resources	2.51	2.3
Utilities	8.24	—
Other	16.66	23.6

1. Includes expenditures for capital improvements.
Sources:
U.S. Bureau of the Census, *1972 Census of Governments*, Vol. 4, No. 5, "Compendium of Government Finances," Table 10.
City of New Haven. *Budget, City of New Haven, Connecticut, 1972-1973.* New Haven, 1972.
City of New Haven, *Budget, City of New Haven, Connecticut, 1974-1975,* New Haven, 1974.

and households and in understanding their relationship to questions of local finance.

Several factors combine to determine the effective property tax rate and the mix of public services provided in a jurisdiction. On the revenue side, the property tax rate varies inversely with the value of taxable property in a jurisdiction for a given level of expenditure. On the expenditure side, the relative importance of the excise component of the local property tax depends upon the relative demand for and costs of supplying public goods and redistribution vis à vis the demand and costs for property related services.

A primary determinant in most cases of the "need" for redistributive programs and of the costs of providing many "pure" public goods is the nature and extent of the poverty population in a jurisdiction. It is therefore significant that poverty and disadvantaged households are heavily concentrated in the central portions of virtually all metropolitan areas. Of course, this concentration is itself nothing new; the central location of low income populations is predicted by traditional economic models of residential location decisions and by the filtering process of housing succession (which suggests that older, more centrally located structures are handed down the income ladder over time). What is relatively new, however, is the political and fiscal separation of these central locations from the rest of the region as defined by its labor and product market.

Table 1-3 indicates the concentration of low income households in selected central cities over the past three decades. For different measures of poverty and for different time periods, the table indicates that a substantially higher fraction of the low income households in each metropolitan area reside within the political boundaries of the central city than in the suburbs. Using the Census definition of poverty, the comparisons for 1970 indicate that the incidence of poverty is typically two or three times as large within central city taxing jurisdictions than in suburban jurisdictions. For the New Haven metropolitan area, the incidence of poverty is more than three times as large in the central city as in the suburbs.

The foregoing analysis helps to explain two trends in the effective tax rates on real property levied in most urban areas—the increased absolute levels of property tax rates, and the substantial differential between the effective tax rates in central cities and in their suburbs. Table 1-4, which presents the effective tax rates in central cities and suburbs for selected metropolitan areas, indicates that the average effective property tax rate may be more than 50 percent higher in typical central cities than in their suburban political jurisdictions.

The set of location incentives generated by such economic forces

Table 1-3. Concentration of Low Income Households in Central Cities for Selected SMSAs, 1950, 1960, 1970.

SMSA	Percent of All Families with Low Incomes In		
	SMSA	Central City	Suburbs
Atlantic City, N.J.			
1950[a]	43.9	51.8	37.1
1960[b]	23.0	33.5	17.3
1970[c]	9.9	16.9	7.5
Baltimore, Md.			
1950	30.2	32.4	24.5
1960	14.5	18.6	9.7
1970	8.5	14.0	4.5
Boston, Ma.			
1950	25.8	31.4	23.1
1960	8.9	16.7	6.2
1970	6.1	11.7	4.5
Chicago, Ill.			
1950	19.6	21.3	16.2
1960	10.6	13.6	6.7
1970	6.8	10.6	3.2
Los Angeles, Calif.			
1950	27.5	29.3	25.9
1960	12.4	14.4	11.3
1970	8.2	9.7	7.0
New Haven, Ct.			
1950	26.8	30.7	20.7
1960	11.6	16.6	7.1
1970	7.3	12.9	4.0
New York, N.Y.			
1950	25.4	28.2	21.0
1960	13.5	15.2	7.4
1970	9.2	11.5	4.2
St. Louis, Mo.			
1950	30.1	33.9	26.0
1960	15.1	21.7	11.4
1970	8.1	14.3	5.9

[a]1950 percent of households with annual incomes below $2,500.

[b]1960 percent of households with annual incomes below $3,000.

[c]1970 percent of households with incomes below the officially designated poverty level.

Sources:

U.S. Bureau of the Census: "Census Tracts." *Census of Population and Housing: 1970.* Final Report PHC(1). Washington, D.C.: U.S. Government Printing Office, 1972. Tables P-1 and P-4.

U.S. Bureau of the Census. "Census Tracts." *Census of Population and Housing: 1960.* Final Report. Washington, D.C.: U.S. Government Printing Office, 1963. Table P-1.

U.S. Bureau of the Census. "Characteristics of the Population." *U.S. Census of Population and Housing: 1950.* Washington, D.C.: U.S. Government Printing Office, 1953. Table 37.

Table 1-4. Average Effective Property Tax Rates in Central City and Suburban Parts of Metropolitan Areas

	Effective Property Tax Rates	
SMSA & Year	*Central City*	*Suburbs*
Atlantic City, N.J.		
1969	5.05	3.45
1973	5.04	3.58
Baltimore, Md.		
1969	2.77	1.45
Boston, Ma.		
1969	12.15	4.78
Newark, N.J.		
1969	7.08	3.74
1973	6.50	3.76
New Haven, Ct.		
1948	3.20	2.30
1960	3.90	2.50
1970	4.50	3.70
1974	4.93	3.41
Trenton, N.J.		
1969	6.63	3.45
1973	6.12	3.22

Sources:
Martin A. Larson and C. Stanley Lowell, *Praise the Lord for Tax Exemptions*, Washington/New York: Robert B. Luce, Inc., 1969.
State of New Jersey, *Annual Report of the Division of Taxation in the Department of the Treasury*. For the fiscal years 1969-1973.
Massachusetts Taxpayers Foundation, Inc., *Institutional Property Tax Exemptions in Massachusetts*, Boston, 1971.
State of Maryland, *Annual Report of Department of Assessments*, various issues.
State of Connecticut, *Quadrennial Statement of Real Estate Exempted from Taxation*, Public Document No. 52, Hartford. Published by the State, various years.
State of Connecticut, *Information Relative to the Assessment and Collection of Taxes*, Public Document No. 48, Hartford. Published by the State, various years.

is almost inescapable. In particular, differential excise rates are difficult—if not impossible—to maintain in the face of factor mobility and factor substitution. Such differentials are even more difficult to maintain when a substantial fraction of households and firms make decisions to move in any year, even if these decisions are caused by exogenous factors such as household demographics or changes in demand for output. In particular, exceptionally higher excises upon real properties quickly give rise to compensating adjustments by producers and consumers to avoid or to minimize these excise burdens. That is, consumers and producers either remove themselves from the locale of the high excise burden or adjust their consumption and production patterns so as to use less real property and more of other goods. The same principle, of course, applies to inefficiencies in the production of those property related services comprising the "service charge" component of the property tax—that is, mobility and substitutability operate to reduce real property usage in localities that are inefficient in the production and distribution of services.

In theory, of course, competitive markets could equalize these excise and service differences across jurisdictions; equilibrium in the long run suggests that property values should modify to capitalize variations in excise burdens and service packages. Decreased demand for highly taxed land in production and consumption should eventually reduce property values, so that variations in the "tax price" for a given level of services will be reduced across jurisdictions. This is, of course, the essence of the economic models of Tiebout and Rothenberg.[9]

Notwithstanding the time lags inherent in this adjustment process, there are also reasons why full capitalization may never occur, even in the long run. If households and firms bidding for sites differ substantially in their ability to shift the burden of property taxation, we may expect a sorting of land use among jurisdictions (just as the federal tax laws lead to a sorting of investment types among income classes).

Since the degree of capitalization depends upon the bid of the marginal individual, variations in "effective" tax rates can lead to relatively little capitalization of "tax prices" across jurisdictions. (Again, the reasoning is identical to the distribution of investment types across income classes: tax exemption for municipal bonds is not fully capitalized into selling prices because the marginal buyer is not in the highest tax bracket.)

Specifically, economic considerations suggest that those who remain, or who choose to compete for sites in high excise jurisdictions, are those who for one reason or another are "immune" from the impact of the high taxes. It thus follows that central cities, which in most metropolitan areas levy relatively high excise rates, increasingly find themselves housing these immune activities. In fact, the extent to which the central cities of most metropolitan areas house these types of activities is striking.

At least three major categories of such immune groups can be identified. The first and most obvious immune category includes tax-exempt institutions and facilities. Of course, such a list begins

with such institutions as universities, schools, churches, and founda-
tions, but it extends well beyond. Other organizations commonly
exempt from local taxation include hospitals, government buildings
(federal and state as well as local), housing authorities, and veterans'
and charitable institutions. In addition, the class of exempt institutions includes bankrupt enterprises (railroad terminals and abandoned
buildings are vivid contemporary examples) and the special "incentive" tax developments used to lure new industry to a town.

Tax exemption is thus not a very limited phenomenon in American cities; in fact roughly one-third of aggregate property values in
American cities is tax exempt for one reason or another.[10] Not
surprisingly, in the light of this analysis, the proportion of tax-
exempt property is substantially higher in central cities than in their
suburban rings and is growing relatively faster in central cities. Table
1-5 indicates the extent of tax exemption in selected central cities
and their suburban rings. The disparity is striking: for 19 of the 22
metropolitan areas for which data are available, the proportion of
property values exempt from local property taxes is higher in the
central city than in the suburbs. In more than half the metropolitan
areas, the proportion of exempt properties is more than twice as
large in the central city as in the suburbs, and in several metropolitan
areas it is more than three times as large.

Beyond legally exempt institutions, there are several other categories of residents insulated from the effects of high excise burdens—for example, those for whom the value of local public outputs
consumed exceeds their tax payments. Among business firms and
enterprises there are likely to be few members of this group. Nevertheless, there are usually a few specialized activities (such as the
manufacture of highly flammable products, the discharge of inordinate
amounts of waste, or the need for special security and protection)
where some firms can compensate for the higher excises in a community through greater service consumption.

But the category of residents most commonly cited as receiving
more in the way of public service than they pay in taxes in central
cities is, of course, the poor. It is argued that the poor particularly
benefit from the better public, medical, and other social services that
are more plentifully supplied in central cities than in the suburbs. In
addition, the central city may provide services in forms that are more
useful and applicable to the problems of the poor. As already noted
(Table 1-3 above), a higher concentration of poor households is
characteristic of central cities—for a variety of reasons besides the
advantages derived from the local public sector.

Still another group with relative immunity from high local excise

Table 1-5. Comparisons of Tax Exempt Real Property in Central Cities and Their Suburban Rings

| SMSA | Year | Percent of All Real Property Exempt | | |
		Central City	*Suburbs*	*State*
Atlantic City, N.J.	1969	20.2	9.6	15.5
Baltimore, Md.	1970	24.8	19.0	22.8
Boston, Ma.	1969	54.2	22.45	—
Bridgeport, Ct.	1969	33.6	12.9	23.7
Denver, Co.	1973	16.1	18.4	20.1
Hartford, Ct.	1969	31.6	16.4	23.7
Jersey City	1969	33.8	14.9	15.5
Lawrence–Haverhill, Ma.	1969	27.8	20.8	—
Minneapolis–St. Paul, Minn.	1968	27.3	17.3	20.5
Newark, N.J.	1969	31.8	14.3	15.5
Newport News–Hampton, Va.	1973	49.1	14.6	17.6
New Haven, Ct.	1969	37.6	13.6	23.7
New London–Norwich, Ct.	1969	41.9	25.9	23.7
New York, N.Y.	1970	34.5	21.4	30.2
Norfolk–Portsmouth	1973	43.0	22.6	17.6
Philadelphia[a]	—	27.3	15.6	23.0
Richmond, Va.	1973	22.2	8.9	17.6
Roanoke, Va.	1973	13.0	22.5	17.6
Springfield–Chicopee–Holyoke, Ma.	1969	27.1	24.0	—
Trenton, N.J.	1969	35.1	36.3	15.5
Washington, D.C.[b]	—	49.8	18.7	—
Worcester, Ma.	1969	37.5	18.3	—

[a]Central city data are for 1971; suburban and state data are for 1969.
[b]Central city percentage is for 1971; suburban percentage includes 1970 data for the two Maryland Counties and 1973 data for the Virginia portion.

Sources:

State of New York, *Statistical Yearbook*, 1972; *Final Report of the Joint Legislative Committee to Study and Investigate Real Property Tax Exemptions*, 1971, Document No. 15.

Massachusetts Taxpayers Foundation, *Institutional Property Tax Exemptions in Massachusetts*, 1971.

State of New Jersey, *Annual Report of the Division of Taxation in the Department of the Treasury.* For the Fiscal Year 1969.

State of Maryland, *Study Commission on the State Tax Structure*, January 4, 1971, p. 247.

State of Virginia, Finance Section of the Division of State Planning and Community Affairs, *Reforming the Virginia Property Tax*, Vol. II. Richmond, 1974.

Barry E. Lipman et al., *Fiscal Prospects and Alternatives: 1974*, A Staff Report to the [Virginia] Revenue Resources and Economic Study Commission, Richmond, Va., June 1973.

Colorado Division of Property Taxation, Department of Local Affairs, *Third Annual Report, 1973*, Denver, 1973.

Pennsylvania Economy League (for the Local Government Commission), "Real Estate Taxes": *A Study of the Financing of Local Government in Pennsylvania*, April 1970.

levies includes those who are able, for one reason or another, to pass along most of their higher taxes to others. For businesses nothing aids such a pass-along quite as much as an inelastic demand for products or services. Among firms, the most obvious examples of activities facing inelastic demand conditions are the public utilities. In fact, a major reason for their public regulation is that such firms are natural monopolies, with inelastic demands for their services. Accordingly, any cost increase resulting from tax rises is normally passed along relatively easily to public utility consumers in the form of higher prices for telephone service, water, and so forth.

Sketchy comparative data, presented in Table 1-6, does suggest that such firms are relatively overrepresented in American central cities. The proportion of workers in selected metropolitan areas classified as "transportation, communication, and public utility workers," does seem higher in central cities than in the suburbs. Unfortunately, it is not possible to separate public utility workers from others in this category. The comparisons between central cities and suburbs do suggest, however, a higher concentration of such activities in central city locations.

Among households, the very rich also are in the position of being relatively immune from local excise levels, although to a more limited extent. Since local taxes are deductible from gross income in computing federal tax liabilities, households in high marginal tax brackets are able to pass on a substantial fraction of local taxes to the federal government. Again, there is some evidence (presented in Table 1-7) that the very rich and the very poor are overrepresented in a selection of central cities with high excise rates as compared with their suburban rings. The table presents the ratio of median to mean in-

International Association of Assessing Officers. Correspondence in the exemptons file on Maryland.

State of Minnesota, *Abstract of Exempt Real Estate*, 1968; Department of Taxation, Research and Planning Division, Biennial Report #16, Table A. 28.

Pennsylvania Economy League (Eastern Division) (with Bureau of Municipal Research), *The Problem of Tax-Exempt Property in Philadelphia*, Report No. 1, 1966.

Pennsylvania League of Cities, *A Survey of Tax-Exempt Real Property in Pennsylvania Cities*, Harrisburg, Pa., July 1, 1971.

State of Connecticut, *Quadrennial Statement of Real Estate Exempted from Taxation, 1970*, Public Document No. 52, Hartford. Published by the State, 1972.

State of Connecticut, *Information Relative to the Assessment and Collection of Taxes, 1971*, Public Document No. 48, Hartford. Published by the State, 1972.

Table 1-6. Concentration of Transportation, Communication, and Utility Workers in Central City and Suburban Locations

SMSA	Percentage of All Workers Employed in Transportation, Communication, and Utility Industries in		
	SMSA	Central City	Suburbs
Baltimore, Md.	6.9	8.9	4.9
Boston, Mass.	6.8	9.6	5.2
Chicago, Ill.	8.2	8.8	7.5
Los Angeles, Calif.	7.1	8.7	5.6
New Haven, Ct.	8.8	11.6	5.4
New York, N.Y.	9.9	11.1	5.9
St. Louis, Mo.	8.1	10.5	6.4

Includes transportation, communication, utilities, sanitary services, and other public utilities.

Source: U.S. Bureau of the Census, *U.S. Census of Population 1970*, "Journey to Work", PC (2)-D, Vol. 2, pt. 6D, Table 2.

Table 1-7. Ratio of Median to Mean Income, for Selected Metropolitan Areas, 1970

SMSA	Ratio of Median to Mean Incomes for Families and Unrelated Individuals		
	SMSA	Central City	Suburbs
Atlantic City, N.J.	.811	.737	.849
Baltimore, Md.	.871	.841	.891
Boston, Ma.	.841	.808	.859
Chicago, Ill.	.877	.858	.891
Los Angeles, Calif.	.822	.769	.881
New Haven, Ct.	.865	.783	.831
New York, N.Y.	.801	.796	.844
St. Louis, Mo.	.881	.821	.897

Sources: U.S. Bureau of the Census, "Census Tracts," *Census of Population and Housing: 1970*, Final Report PHC(1), Washington, D.C.: U.S. Government Printing Office, 1972. Tables P-1 and P-4.

comes for central cities and suburbs for selected metropolitan areas. This ratio is larger for suburban areas in each of the comparisons, indicating a more internally egalitarian distribution of income in the suburban rings.

Given all this potential slippage between the imposition and collection of local taxes, it is clear why adjustment to long run equilibrium through changes in property values is sluggish in many metropolitan areas. Besides barriers to short run adjustment due to imperfect substitution between land and other factors, growing populations of immune activities will inhibit price adjustment. An expanding sector of tax-exempt properties, or the immigration of poverty households (particularly minority groups, who may face other restrictions on where they may settle in the metropolitan area) can maintain property values above the equilibrium levels implied by full capitalization possibly indefinitely.

In summary, several clearly identifiable trends resulting from technical change in transportation, communications, and production processes have substantially increased the substitutability of alternative production sites in the typical metropolitan area. These same factors have greatly reduced the importance of accessibility to the core of metropolitan areas as a motivation for households' choices of residential sites. At the same time, reliance upon property taxes to finance local public output has continued, while the levels of local taxation have increased. When combined with transport and other improvements, these trends have greatly increased the importance of tax and public services in influencing the site choices of both firms and households.

In general, those portions of metropolitan areas with relatively high excise levies against property, particularly central cities, are found to attract firms and households which are relatively insensitive or immune to these higher taxes. These forces operate to a greater or lesser extent in most of urban America. However, these factors are far more important quantitatively in a certain class of metropolitan areas—namely those of small to medium size (especially where the central city is a limited portion of the metropolitan area), those that have older housing stocks and infrastructures, those that are growing slowly or declining in population and output, and those with a multiplicity of jurisdictions.

In smaller metropolitan areas, transport cost differentials are smaller in absolute magnitude and relatively less important in motivating the locational choices of firms and households. Smaller metropolitan areas are also those where external economies of scale and agglomeration are presumably less important. Older metropolitan areas, particularly those with older stocks of centrally located residential housing, are those where the central concentrations of disadvantaged households tend to be greatest, and where the potential variation in the excise component of site levies may be quite pronounced. Similarly, metropolitan areas containing more political jurisdictions have more potential for variation in tax rates, in public services and in relative efficiencies of public service production.

We may thus expect that the policy problems facing the central cities in this class of metropolitan area are particularly acute. The basic issues for economic policy facing decision makers in these central cities can be framed in two questions.

1. How can the base upon which tax revenues are raised be increased? In particular, can it be raised in such a way that the adverse location consequences for the central city can be alleviated without undue sacrifices in economic efficiency?

2. How can the efficiency of production of local services be increased? In particular, can efficiencies in production, in combination with alternative pricing structures, be devised so that the consequences of these trends can be alleviated?

The remainder of this volume is devoted to evaluating these policy issues for a single city, which we believe to be reasonably typical of the class of heavily impacted, old, medium-sized, central cities. Specifically, with only one exception, the analyses that follow address these issues using the city of New Haven as a case study. As the data in Tables 1-1 through 1-7 have suggested, the situation in New Haven is highly typical of the public finance problems and the locational incentives facing other American cities.

In broadest outline, the first part of this volume (Chapters Two through Four) addresses the first of these questions: How might local tax revenues be increased without sacrificing efficiency? The second part (Chapters Five through Seven) is concerned with the second question: How might the efficiency of public service delivery be improved? Obviously these two issues are not mutually exclusive, and their resolution—economic efficiency in the allocation of resources and productive efficiency in the utilization of resources—is the implicit though elusive goal of much of the urban policy debate. Chapter Eight provides a concluding comment and summary of findings.

Expanding the Tax Base

✱ *Chapter 2*

Prospects for Economic Development:
The New Haven Case

Malcolm Getz
Robert A. Leone

THE NATURE OF ECONOMIC DEVELOPMENT

The development of a local economy means jobs, prestige, wealth, and tax revenues. Public policies to stimulate local economies are therefore politically attractive at all levels of government. For older cities, like New Haven, perhaps these policies should be called "redevelopment" programs, since their main purpose is to help an area during a period of major economic transition. For example, the demise of the textile industry in the industrial Northeast has forced many cities to adopt development strategies to attract growth industries to fill vacant mill space. The growth of Digital Equipment Corporation in the abandoned mills of Maynard, Massachusetts, is a classic example.

In practice, economic growth can benefit certain socioeconomic groups more than others, and growth can utilize resources for certain uses instead of others. Thus, an economic development program deals implicitly with issues of equity and economic efficiency. Since economic development programs may be advocated for local as well as national reasons, it is important to recognize the possible contradictions. Policies motivated by national objectives may cause losses in local economic welfare. And policies advocated for local purposes may cause national losses in welfare.

Eliminating contradictions in development policies alone will not result in effective control of the direction a local economy should take. Market forces are continually moving an economy, and these forces are likely to be much stronger than any development policy, particularly one formulated at the local level. A prime example of a current that will be difficult to oppose is the suburbanization of employment. Changes in production technologies, in transportation networks, in consumer incomes, and increases in space requirements cause continuing movements of employment, especially manufacturing employment, to suburban areas. Market forces creating the tide of suburbanization are unlikely to be abated by any local or national policy. Central city development programs that see their goal as stemming the growth of suburban employment are not likely to be successful. Development policies in central cities that both accept the market forces leading to suburbanization and seek to exploit the continuing comparative advantages of the central city will be both cheaper to administer and more successful in achieving their limited, but more readily attainable, goals.

In addition to the constraints of the marketplace are legal constraints and the existence of aging buildings. The legal construction of a local government limits the varieties of taxes it may impose: it has almost no power to regulate directly jobs or capital; and it may even be relatively limited in its ability to shape government activity within its own boundaries. For example, it is often the case that highways, which are so important to a locality's economic prospects, are planned at the state level with surprisingly little local input. The existence of older buildings frequently implies a lack of readily available vacant land. The prospects for local growth policies under these conditions may be limited.

THE DEVELOPMENT ISSUES
FOR NEW HAVEN

In this chapter the specifics of growth and change in the New Haven economy are considered, and prospects for economic development are defined. Throughout, we seek to understand the economic forces that are shaping New Haven and propose policies that move with the economic tide. Moreover, we identify policies that aim at national as well as local gains by reducing market inefficiencies. And we adopt the equity stance that changes that improve the lot of low income people are desirable. Changes in employment levels within the city of New Haven are compared with changes in surrounding suburban towns. The movement of firms within the New Haven area are tracked, and the results of some interviews with firms that have moved in the last five years are presented. We conclude that while economic development is unlikely to be of much help with the city's fiscal problem, it may have some value for long term efficiency and equity gains.

Like many other cities which are constrained to finance municipal government by the property tax, the city of New Haven has placed a high priority on its economic development program in the expectation that successful policies will expand the tax base and consequently reduce the pressures for higher tax rates. Given the reality of existing market forces, and New Haven's geographic limitations, it is not clear that such an objective is attainable. It is also not clear that such an objective, even if attainable, is desirable. For example, development will almost surely change the demand for city services. If new employment attracts low-skilled workers, the demand for services may be large. Clearly, the net fiscal impact of development is the relevant criterion if policies are to have fiscal objectives. Similarly, a policy to allow only skilled employment in capital-intensive industry may assure additions to property tax revenues and only minimal increases in public service demands, but it may be quite inconsistent with improving the income of current city residents. The need for a development policy thus should be carefully considered.

Given, however, that economic development is deemed desirable, then a development strategy has to be chosen. An important issue in that choice is whether to exploit further some particular comparative advantage a city has over other urban areas or to diversify the local economic base. There are arguments for and against both approaches. In the past, the city of New Haven exploited its geographic location and became a major rail hub in the Northeast corridor. The railroad was for many years a major source of tax revenue to the city. Today the rail industry is declining, the facilities are deteriorating physically, and much of its real estate has been made tax exempt. Old advantages may not indicate current opportunities. Today, if New Haven were to attempt to exploit its transportation advantage, rather than focusing on rail, it might emphasize the port facility. Expenditures on harbor improvements might attract industries such as oil refining needing an outlet to the sea.

A diversified industrial base has several advantages. According to Benjamin Chinitz,[1] lack of industrial diversification has important implications for economic growth and adjustment of the urban economy over time. He observes that in a diversified area, trucking, communications, and business services are more likely to be provided by small independent firms than by large corporations. This facilitates the entry of new smaller firms, which may be an important stimulus to growth in the long run: as one part of the economy slackens, new industries replace the declining ones. If an area is specialized, however, a decline in its predominant industry can be catastrophic. Thus, from a dynamic point of view, a more diverse economy is less subject to economic fluctuations: economic diversity, by its nature, sustains itself.

At present the New Haven area is relatively diversified. In an examination by Ullman, Dacey, and Brodsky[2] of the nation's 101 largest SMSAs, New Haven ranked 59th in employment concentration by industry. By comparison, neighboring Bridgeport had the seventh most highly concentrated urban economy in the United States, and Hartford the 20th. This suggests that a diversification objective may already have been achieved in New Haven. Consequently, a development program aimed primarily at fiscal objectives can safely place a lower priority on diversification needs.

But there is a more perplexing choice confronting the city: should it emphasize growth and change within its boundaries, or should it promote the development of the whole metropolitan area? When city planners see firms moving from within city boundaries to suburban locations, it is easy to conclude that the city and the suburbs are in competition for employment and tax revenues. Contrary to popular belief, however, 1970 Census information for New Haven clearly indicates that job opportunities in the suburbs are quite accessible to central city residents, including poor and disadvantaged ethnic groups, although suburban residential opportunities may be limited.

To determine the mobility of New Haven's work force, we looked at the Census tracts in the city where either: (1) the percentage of black population is more than the average for the city; (2) the median and mean incomes are at least $1,000 less than that for the city as a whole; (3) the median years of education are less than those for the city; or (4) substantial Italian population is present (the last category is included because Italians are cited in several interviews as an important source of local semiskilled labor). Typically, 30 percent of the poor, black, and Italian workers who live in New Haven work outside the city.

Since city residents can successfully commute to the suburbs, it is not necessary to increase the number of jobs within the city boundaries to aid city residents. The greater the mobility of the labor force in the metropolitan area, the more the area may be viewed as a single labor market. City development strategists should perhaps focus on increasing employment throughout the metropolitan area. This focus need not conflict with fiscal objectives, at least.in the long run. For example, the city of New Haven is a retail and communications center for financial, utility, and commercial establishments. A good number of these service activities that find the central city location attractive will grow if the surrounding region thrives economically.

The market forces leading to the suburbanization of employment within urban areas are deep-rooted. Given labor mobility, and the fact that some central employment may be induced by economic growth in the suburbs, a metropolitan-wide development focus seems warranted in the New Haven context. Policies that would seek to develop the city at the expense of its surrounding suburbs may be unwise.

In planning economic development, strategists for New Haven might keep in mind that although the city presently finances its municipal services through the property tax, perhaps that will change. Thus, it may also be unwise for the city to pursue strategies which will serve solely to increase the property tax base. Of more vital long run importance may be the provision of jobs for city residents, particularly those limited in their residential mobility. As long as residential discrimination exists in the suburbs, the job problem for the city will grow along with its minority population.

ECONOMIC CHANGE AND DEVELOPMENT PROSPECTS IN NEW HAVEN

We now focus our attention on the development prospects of the city of New Haven. By examining recent changes in this city's economy, we hope to identify specific policies consistent with the entire area's needs. The objective is to illustrate the importance of prevailing local conditions and their effect on the formulation of any local development program. The analysis covers the years 1967-1971, a period of boom as well as recession.

Change in the Manufacturing Sector

Table 2-1 summarizes changes in the number of manufacturing establishments by municipality within the New Haven SMSA. Establishments which relocated *within the SMSA* between 1967 and 1971 are defined as "Movers" in the table. Newly founded establishments and establishments which moved into the SMSA from outside are called "Births." "Deaths" include both establishments that ceased to do business, as well as those that emigrated from the New Haven SMSA. All other establishments are "Non-movers."

The changes documented in the table are quite substantial. The city of New Haven, for example, has the highest proportion of non-moving manufacturing establishments (75 percent of the 1971 total, versus an average of 65 percent in the rest of the SMSA). The city of New Haven was the only significant loser due to out-migration by manufacturing establishments. More optimistically, it should be noted that 53 establishments in the SMSA making relocation deci-

Table 2-1. New Haven SMSA Manufacturing Establishments: Movers, Non-Movers, Births, and Deaths, by Municipality, 1967-1971

	SMSA	Branford	East Haven	Guilford	Hamden	New Haven	North Branford	North Haven	Orange	West Haven
Non-movers										
Total	613	24	14	24	84	295	7	73	28	64
Movers										
Origins	140	8	3	0	18	82	4	12	2	11
Destinations	140	11	5	3	30	53	3	13	6	16
Births	126	11	5	11	22	44	1	13	7	12
Deaths										
Total	113	13	5	3	17	52	0	12	2	9
Establishments:										
1967	866	45	22	27	119	429	11	97	32	84
1971	879	46	24	38	136	392	11	99	41	92
Net Change										
1967-71	+13	+1	+2	+11	+17	-37	0	+2	+9	+8

More precisely, the time period covered by this and other tables based on the Dun and Bradstreet data sources is July 1967 to December 1971.

Source: J. Daykin, N. Haight, and A. Stevens, *Developing the New Haven Economy*, a 1972 Report of the Summer Interns in Economic Development to the New England Board of Higher Education, Wellesley, Mass., pp. 23, 26.

sions during this period chose to locate in New Haven. Although most of these moves were between two points within the city, it is important to emphasize that a large number of establishments specifically chose *not* to move out of New Haven even though they wished to relocate. Movers seem to be relatively more important to the city of New Haven than to any neighboring jurisdiction.

Since expansion is the single most important factor causing an establishment to relocate, any economic development program for the city of New Haven might well place a high priority on satisfying the expanding space requirements of firms already located in the city. Given the small scale of these relocating enterprises, it might suggest real estate referral services that attempt to link growing enterprises with space vacated by less successful firms. Given the important imperfections in the real estate market related to price regulations, etc., these valuable brokerage services may not be profitable for the private sector.

Table 2-1 also indicates that a large proportion of new economic enterprises (34.9 percent) locate in New Haven. This is not surprising, of course, since many young firms need the advantages of more numerous business contacts and services and the proximity to suppliers that the city can offer. The attractiveness of the central city for new economic enterprises suggests that the city of New Haven might exploit its role as an "incubator" of new businesses. In this role, the city might serve as liaison between small businesses and public and private sources of venture capital.

Table 2-2 shows the number of manufacturing establishments that moved from each town within the SMSA to each of the others. It shows rather dramatically the exodus of economic activity from the central city. Only the city of New Haven shows a significant loss in the number of manufacturing establishments due to emigration.

Change in Individual Industries

Since emigration from the central city is a serious concern for New Haven, or for any city, these moves can be analyzed in more detail. A breakdown by industry (not shown in the tables) indicates that the nonelectrical machinery industry is the most active in terms of total relocations, but is not the only industry in which New Haven has sustained significant losses. Losses are also prevalent in apparel, printing and publishing, furniture and fixtures, and electrical equipment and suppliers.

The departure of several large apparel manufacturers from New Haven comes rather unexpectedly, since apparel accounts for most of the city's new industries (Table 2-3). The number of new apparel

Table 2-2.   Origins and Destinations of Manufacturing Relocations, 1967–1971

Town of Origin	Town of Destination										Total Moves[a] Originating in the Town Named at Left
	Branford	East Haven	Guilford	Hamden	New Haven	North Branford	North Haven	Orange	West Haven	Outside SMSA	
Branford	6	0	0	0	1	1	0	0	0	0	8
East Haven	0	2	1	0	0	0	0	0	0	0	3
Guilford	0	0	0	0	1	0	0	0	0	0	1
Hamden	1	1	0	12	1	0	1	0	0	0	16
New Haven	2	1	1	15	43	1	9	2	7	1	82
North Branford	1	0	0	1	1	0	0	0	0	1	4
North Haven	0	1	0	2	2	3	0	2	2	0	12
Orange	0	0	0	0	0	0	0	0	1	1	2
West Haven	1	0	0	0	0	0	0	1	6	3	11
Outside SMSA	0	0	1	0	5	0	0	1	3	0	10
Total Moves Terminating in Town Named at Head of Column	11	5	3	30	53	3	13	6	19	6	149

[a]See Table 2–3 note.

Source: Daykin, Haight and Stevens, *op. cit.* p. 26.

Table 2-3.   Births in Manufacturing Industries, New Haven SMSA, 1967–1971

SIC Code	Industry	Under 20 Employees		20 and Over Employees		
		New Haven	SMSA Outside City	New Haven	SMSA Outside City	Total
19	Ordnance	0	0	0	0	0
20	Food	2	1	1	1	5
22	Textile	1	0	0	0	1
23	Apparel	5	3	6	1	15
24	Lumber	0	2	0	0	2
25	Furniture	3	1	0	0	4
26	Paper	0	1	0	1	2
27	Print. & Pub.	5	6	0	1	12
28	Chemicals	1	3	0	1	5
29	Petroleum	0	0	0	0	0
30	Rubber & Plas.	2	2	0	0	4
31	Leather	0	0	0	1	1
32	Stone, Clay, Glass	0	2	0	0	2
33	Primary Metals	2	2	0	0	4
34	Fab. Metals	3	9	1	1	14
35	Mach. (nonelec.)	6	8	0	2	16
36	Elec. Equip.	1	5	0	1	7
37	Trans. Equip.	2	1	0	0	3
38	Instruments	2	5	0	1	8
39	Misc. Mfg.	2	4	0	0	6
	Total	37	55	8	11	111

Note: Excludes 14 in-migrants to the SMSA classified as "Births" in Table 2-2.
Source: Daykin, Haight and Stevens, op. cit., p. 20.

establishments suggests that conditions for this industry relative to the surrounding area are extremely favorable. This implies that during an apparel firm's formative years, when it has a small clientele and recruits skilled labor, a central city location is of great value. As it grows in size and reputation, the need for larger quarters and better transportation outlets encourages it to move to a suburban location, where it is still able to retain a good portion of its original labor force.

Apparel firms supply 4,000 jobs in New Haven (4,528 in the SMSA), comprising 18.6 percent of the city's manufacturing employment. The industry's significant position in the life of the city is further reinforced by a finding of Ullman, Dacey, and Brodsky.[3] They observe that nondurable manufacturing, of which the apparel industry is a major part, comprises 18.1 percent of the SMSA's total production for markets outside the metropolitan area. It is these so-called "export" markets that fuel local economic growth. Clearly, apparel is a key industry within the manufacturing sector. To slow the exodus of large apparel establishments from the city, development strategists might encourage manpower programs to insure an adequate training of the central city labor force. It might also be the case, however, that a program to actively seek the retention of low paying jobs in the apparel industry may conflict with the fiscal objectives of a development program, since low income workers tend to reside in the city, and they tend to have disproportionately high public service needs.

Printing and publishing (27), another nondurable manufacturing industry, also shows a high degree of mobility. Again, this is an industry in which a relatively large number of new firms have been forming, both in the city and the region, although they tend on the average to be smaller than the young apparel firms. Fifty of the SMSA's 96 printers and publishers are located within New Haven. Although these 50 provide employment for 1,468 people (6.8 percent of the city's manufacturing jobs), 35 of the establishments employ fewer than ten persons. Given their small average size and geographical dispersion within the SMSA, it is reasonable to conclude that these printing facilities serve a primarily local clientele and not markets outside the SMSA. Printing and publishing does not, then, present a difficult policy area; there are other industries in which development efforts can reap more significant rewards.

Durable manufacturing is a cause for greater concern, since it comprises 33.7 percent of the city's total employment and produces for markets outside the SMSA. As the most important single component of this export sector, any significant outward movement of establishments in this group is cause for alarm. Among durable manufacturing industries, furniture and fixtures (25), nonelectrical machinery (35), and electrical equipment and supplies (36) have displayed the most outward movement. Unlike the industries discussed above, furniture is not characterized by a high "birth" rate. Less than half (13) the SMSA's 27 furniture manufacturers are located in New Haven. Eight of the New Haven firms employ less than ten persons, while larger firms (20 to 100 employees) are more often found elsewhere in the SMSA. This appears to be part of a trend.

As Table 2-4 indicates, establishments employing over twenty persons are leaving the central city in relatively large numbers. These facts again fit our incubator hypothesis: as an establishment grows in size, the expense of remaining in the city outweighs any advantages of a central location. In this instance we observe that the larger furniture manufacturers are tending to group themselves in a particular sector of the SMSA, perhaps because they can continue to enjoy easy access to the same suppliers.

A similar pattern emerges for nonelectrical machinery. While there are many births (the largest number of any manufacturing industry in the SMSA), these births tend to be small establishments locating outside of New Haven. And, the departure of older machinery manufacturers from the city represents the largest manufacturers contemplating expansion (this would include many of the births); space constraints rule out a New Haven location. The relatively even spatial distribution of the SMSA's 114 machinery establishments (36 in New Haven, 22 in Hamden, 18 in West Haven, 13 in Branford, 12 in North Haven, and 13 in the remaining area towns) reinforces this hypothesis. Twenty-six of those in New Haven employ less than ten people, while those employing over twenty are most frequently found elsewhere in the SMSA, often in Hamden.

The case of the electrical equipment and supplies industry is similar. Moves and births here are less frequent, but the births that do occur are nearly all outside New Haven. Of the SMSA's 40 electrical equipment manufacturing firms, 12 are located in New Haven, 12 in Hamden, 9 in North Haven, and 7 in other communities. As a general rule, the larger the firm, the less likely it is to be found within the city; as a result, only a small portion (615) of the SMSA's 3,353 electrical equipment manufacturing jobs are in New Haven.

Nonmanufacturing Employment

New Haven, like many other U.S. central cities, has experienced a striking increase in nonmanufacturing employment, with the largest gains taking place in the service and government sectors. This growth

Table 2-4. Movers in Manufacturing Industries, New Haven SMSA, 1967-1971, by Industry and Establishment Size

| | | Under 20 Employees | | | | 20 and Over Employees | | | | Total No. of Moves |
| | | New Haven Moves | | | Moves Within SMSA, Not Involving New Haven | New Haven Moves | | | Moves Within SMSA, Not Involving New Haven | |
SIC Code	Industry	Into City	Out of City	Within City		Into City	Out of City	Within City		
19	Ordnance	0	0	0	1	0	1	1	1	4
20	Food	1	1	0	1	0	0	0	1	4
22	Textile	0	1	0	0	0	1	1	1	4
23	Apparel	0	0	0	0	0	3	5	1	9
24	Lumber	0	0	0	1	0	0	1	1	3
25	Furniture	0	1	2	4	1	4	1	0	13
26	Paper	0	0	0	0	0	1	0	1	2
27	Print. & Pub.	0	1	6	3	0	2	1	0	13
28	Chemicals	1	0	1	1	0	2	1	0	6
29	Petroleum	0	0	0	3	0	0	0	1	4
30	Rubber & Plastics	0	0	3	0	1	1	1	2	8
31	Leather	0	0	0	0	0	0	0	0	0
32	Stone, Clay, Glass	0	0	1	1	2	0	1	1	6
33	Primary Metals	0	0	0	1	0	1	1	1	6
34	Fab. Metals	0	1	0	2	0	1	0	2	18
35	Mach. (non-elec.)	2	0	3	6	0	1	2	5	29
36	Elec. Equip.	3	7	1	9	0	2	2	6	9
37	Trans. Equip.	0	0	0	3	0	0	2	1	3
38	Instruments	1	0	1	0	0	0	1	1	3
39	Misc. Mfg.	0	2	4	2	0	0	0	0	8
	Total	9	14	23	38	4	20	19	25	152

Note: Moves into and out of the SMSA not involving the City of New Haven are excluded here. The definitions of "Movers" for this table include 12 moves into or out of the SMSA reported as "Births" and "Deaths," respectively, in Table 2-2.

Source: Daykin, Haight and Stevens, op. cit., p. 19.

is especially encouraging, since these industries all have a high labor component. As a consequence, growth in these industries has a highly favorable local economic impact. A high percentage of nonmanufacturing employment produces for markets outside the SMSA. Within the nonmanufacturing sector, professional services and transportation, communication, and utilities stand out as the most obvious sectors for study because they provide a large number of these stimulative "export" jobs.

Table 2–5, however, shows these industries to be changing very little. Their importance can no doubt be attributed largely to the size of two particular exporters—Conrail and Yale University. On the one hand, neither Yale nor the railroad is likely to move or to go out of business, so the city need not worry about preventing these occurrences; on the other hand, given the current financial condition of these two institutions, neither of them is likely to expand in direct response to city policy. The city can, however, provide a climate more or less favorable to expansion.

In Conrail's case, for example, the city might be in a position to assist the railroad in the development of, say, a piggyback trailer terminal. Piggybacking remains a significant growth activity in the railroad industry. Conrail may be able to finance trailers relatively easily via lease arrangement, but initial capital constraints may make it difficult for the railroad to improve its terminal facilities. A public policy of terminal development might be consistent with the city's needs, the railroad's capabilities, and the transportation demands of the high density industrial Northeast.

Construction and wholesaling activities rank somewhat lower in absolute importance than transportation and education, but are experiencing more births and moves. Are these sectors more promising policy targets? The answer appears to be negative.

The construction industry, including general, heavy construction, and special trades contractors, is not heavily concentrated in the city of New Haven. Only 31.8 percent of the SMSA's 550 contractors employing over twenty persons are located within New Haven. Except for special trade contractors (important in Hamden and West Haven), these firms show a remarkably even geographic distribution. It appears that, for this particular industry, a central city location is not an important advantage. The problems posed by lack of space available at appropriate prices in the city undoubtedly discourage businesses such as these, which require a large area for storage of materials and equipment. Construction, then, does not appear to be a sector that can be counted upon to play a major role in any economic development program; in fact, given its land requirements, it

Table 2-5.   Births and Movers in Nonmanufacturing Industries, New Haven SMSA, 1967–1971, 20 and Over Employees

SIC Code	Industry	Births		Movers			
		New Haven	SMSA Outside City	Into City	Out of City	Within City	Within SMSA, Not Involving City
01	Livestock	0	2	0	0	0	0
15	Gen. Bldg.	1	3	0	0	1	0
16	Heavy Constr.	2	1	0	0	0	0
17	Spec. Trade	0	2	0	2	0	0
42	Truck & Warehouse	1	2	0	0	0	0
48	Communications	0	1	0	0	0	0
50	Wholesale Trade	4	9	0	11	1	3
52	Bldg. Materials	0	2	0	0	0	0
53	Gen. Merchandise	1	3	0	0	0	0
54	Food Stores	1	1	0	0	0	0
55	Auto Dealers	2	0	0	0	1	0
56	Apparel Stores	1	0	1	0	0	1
57	Furn. Stores	0	0	1	0	0	0
58	Eat. & Drink	9	11	1	0	1	0
59	Misc. Retail	0	2	0	1	1	0
67	Holding Co.	1	2	0	0	0	0
70	Hotels	2	1	0	0	2	0
72	Pers. Services	0	0	0	0	1	0
73	Misc. Bus. Ser.	1	1	0	1	1	0
75	Auto Repair	0	1	0	0	1	0
76	Misc. Reapir	1	0	0	0	0	0
79	Amusement	0	1	0	0	0	0
80	Med. & Health	1	0	0	0	0	0
89	Misc. Services	0	1	0	0	0	0
	Total	28	46	2	15	8	4

Source: Daykin, Haight and Stevens, op. cit., p. 21.

may even be most rational for the city to discourage this type of industry.

Wholesaling establishments employing over twenty persons (of which there are 556 in the SMSA and 267 in New Haven) are leaving the city. New establishments in this sector are also choosing to locate elsewhere, apparently failing to see the central city location as an advantage in the early stages of their business and finding transportation facilities elsewhere in the SMSA to be excellent. As the city of New Haven would probably prefer more labor intensive uses of its scarce land resources, this decline in wholesaling is neither surprising nor discouraging.

Two more promising development alternatives exist in the non-manufacturing sector. One relates to research and science-based service industries. New Haven is home to a substantial medical complex and could thus serve as a modest base for more life–study service related endeavors. Another opportunity lies with headquarters operations. The creep of headquarters relocations out of New York City and up the Connecticut coast could, with time and some encouragement, extend all the way to New Haven. The opportunity is worth exploring, especially considering New Haven's reputation as an urbane city.

In sum, it should be noted that although services and other non-manufacturing industries are the most rapidly growing segment of the New Haven economy, and provide some intriguing possibilities for New Haven's future, manufacturing industries must be counted upon to play a crucial role in the city's economic development strategy. The reasons are twofold: manufacturing industries still dominate the "export" sector, and they appear more susceptible to the city development policy.

A PERSPECTIVE ON
RELOCATING
PLANTS

Since industry relocations are an important part of the changing New Haven economy, the managements of 33 establishments relocating in the New Haven area were interviewed, as well as several government officials. The results reflect perceptions of the New Haven economy held by the business community. All establishments interviewed employed at least twenty persons, had moved within the past five years, and served markets outside the SMSA.

Questions concerning space were emphasized, since it was widely believed that establishments moved out of the city when they could not find large tracts of land (at prices they could afford) upon which to build new plants. The interviews indicated that the need for more space was indeed the primary reason for moving. Of the 33 establishments that moved, 45 percent were prompted by the need for additional space. Among the establishments moving to larger quarters, the majority moved out of the city. Several employers who moved out of the city cited the lack of adequate warehousing space in the city; others simply said it was no longer necessary to be located in the central business district. Some felt that all the available existing plants in New Haven were outmoded and would be too costly to use.

A second reason for moves was high taxes. Many employers felt that land costs in New Haven were too high and property taxes were excessive. One owner who considered a Long Wharf site (a prime city-owned waterfront redevelopment area) abandoned the idea when he considered his future tax payments to be prohibitive. The larger establishments which required greater amounts of space found the tax and property costs most burdensome.

Not all the establishments requiring more space moved out of New Haven. Of the ten establishments that moved within the City, half moved to obtain more space. But, among these, only one built a new plant; the others bought existing buildings. Two of these were apparel manufacturers using fairly old structures. Such operations were typically located in building lofts and required small amounts of space. A central site was relatively inexpensive and provided easy access for employees who were easily trained. One employer also pointed out that New Haven was a good location for the apparel industry since many supply warehouses were also located in the city. Three nonmanufacturers remained in New Haven in order to be close to their clientele. The nonmanufacturing establishments felt New Haven was a central location, thus providing them with the largest possible market in the SMSA. Like the apparel manufacturers, these establishments were also located near their suppliers. In general, then, New Haven is still perceived as a good business location by many business persons.

All employers interviewed indicated that finding suitable employees at different locations presented no problem. Not only was labor generally available, but unskilled labor was found to be much more mobile than expected. Although very few unskilled laborers might be expected to stay with establishments moving to areas where there was no public transportation, interviews showed this not to be the case. Although all the firms that moved to North Haven and Branford (suburban towns with interstate access) commented that lack of public transportation was an inconvenience, their workers still found ways to get to work. In only one case, involving an establishment that moved to Orange (a town about eight miles from New Haven's central business district) did the employer comment on the loss of help due to the move.

With some exceptions, wages in the New Haven area were generally perceived to be lower than in other parts of the state. While the apparel industry employers thought that wages in this area were high, in most other industries employing unskilled workers, employers indicated that wages were low. Throughout the SMSA, wage rates seemed to remain uniform. No employer attributed an increase or decrease in wage payments to a change in location.

Because New Haven has undergone so much redevelopment in the past decade, many of the establishments that moved may have done so only because they were forced to by redevelopment. Of those interviewed, five employers cited redevelopment as the primary reason for moving. Although it might be reasonable to expect that firms that had been forced to move would be resentful toward the city, most of the firms believed the new construction to be advantageous and expressed no resentment about their forced move. The people most dissatisfied were those who had been forced to move due to proposed construction that never took place. In all cases the employers felt the city, through the Redevelopment Agency, had tried as hard as it could to find them a new site, but that the alternative locations the Agency had suggested were inadequate and, in most cases, simply too small.

Employers who came to the city government to seek help in relocating to a larger tract of land felt that the city had been inadequate in its aid. It was clear that aid was not forthcoming in most circumstances because the sites were simply not available within the city. In contrast, a number of firms cited the good working relationships that existed between them and their suburban governments. Most employers interviewed indicated that the town they moved into had aided them in their search for a new location. Hamden and North Haven, for example, have economic industrial commissions to encourage business to locate in their towns. In addition, eleven establishments considered crime a problem in New Haven, and most mentioned vandalism as their specific concern. Two firms listed crime as their primary reason for moving, and those who had moved farther from the center of the city felt that the crime problem was less severe in their new location.

It is often suggested that New Haven has a distinct transportation advantage over other areas in the SMSA, for the city is served by two major interstate highways and is a major rail hub. Further, New

Haven has both a port and an airport. Yet, other cities and towns in the SMSA, although not near a group of major transportation facilities, are close to at least one major facility. North Haven is located on Interstate 91. Guilford, Branford, East Haven, West Haven, and Orange are all located on Interstate 95. All the cities and towns in the SMSA except the bedroom communities of Woodbridge, Bethany, North Branford, and Orange have railroad service. A noncommercial highway, the Wilbur Cross Parkway, services Orange, Hamden, and Woodbridge, as well as New Haven. Although not useful for trucking, it is convenient for employees driving to work.

A majority of the interviewees moved to North Haven. All of them felt that transportation for their goods was better in North Haven than it had been in New Haven, as trucks could easily get from Interstate 91 to their plants. A large number of firms also moved to West Haven. Again it was easier for trucks to reach their plants than it had been in their New Haven location. The establishments that moved to Hamden did not consider transportation a major problem, although there is no major interstate highway there. The only major highway passing through the town is the Wilbur Cross, which trucks cannot use. An often cited transportation factor was the ease of access between plant and highway, and the suburban areas do very well in this regard.

SUMMARY OBSERVATIONS

Three basic observations summarize recent changes in economic activity in the New Haven area. First, the total number of jobs in the city of New Haven has increased by 3,420 or 5.3 percent since 1960. Manufacturing jobs, however, have not grown in the metropolitan area since 1960 and have actually declined by 14 percent in New Haven, although they still constitute 31 percent of all jobs in the city. Nonmanufacturing employment in the city has increased by 26 percent since 1960, more than offsetting losses in the manufacturing sector. The fastest growing local industry is services, including nonprofit institutions: services have grown by 16 percent in the past five years.

Second, economic activity is shifting outward. In 1970, 56 percent of all area jobs were in the city, versus 67 percent in 1960. This spatial change is primarily the net result of higher growth rates for suburban versus central city firms. Since 1967, employment in suburban manufacturing firms grew 37 percent faster than central city manufacturing employment. The movement of firms from New Haven to its suburbs has contributed to this outward shift of jobs.

Fifty-four "export" sector firms have moved from New Haven to its suburbs since 1967, while only twelve such firms have moved into the city. In the last five years no large manufacturing firm has moved from the city to a site outside the metropolitan area.

And third, the city serves as an incubator for new business enterprises. Of 185 new business formations in the New Haven area since 1967, 40 percent were located in the city. This phenomenon is especially noticeable in the apparel and printing and publishing industries.

Several policy implications follow. First, the lack of vacant land and the high cost of existing space is the most important constraint on economic growth in New Haven. Fifteen of 33 firms interviewed cited the lack of space as their primary reason for moving out of the city. Any economic development program thus might give priority to satisfying these expanding space requirements. Unfortunately, this may be virtually impossible to do in older central cities.

Alternatively, the city might exploit its role as an incubator of new business enterprises by: (1) conserving low cost, easily divisible manufacturing loft space; (2) providing liaison between small business managers and public and private sources of venture capital; and (3) maintaining an up-to-date directory of available space.

The city might also attempt to exploit its comparative advantage in providing services in several ways. For example, the city might seek additional hospitals and medical research facilities. These facilities are often government supported and frequently their locations are determined by political as opposed to economic criteria. Possibly New Haven could become a self-sustaining national medical research center in addition to meeting the growing health care needs of the region. To complement political efforts, the city could implement paraprofessional vocational training programs, especially in the medical and legal areas. In addition, the city could better coordinate and accommodate expansion of the local public and private educational complex.

Finally, the city might acknowledge that the growth of newspapers, television, and telephone firms—all important central city employers—depends upon the growth of the metropolitan area. The importance of these industries is a strong argument for implementing a regional development policy.

The city needs *all* its existing firms, both large and small. Many small firms that had moved out of the city commented that the city government had not helped them to remain within the city. When urban renewal took their locations, the firms felt that the city was often unable or unwilling to find new locations. The feeling persists among small employers that the city government is interested only in large, prestigious firms. To improve its communication with the whole business community, the city might designate a specific governmental agency to respond to the problems and inquiries of the business community.

The policies identified here, if pursued, would not dramatically alter the economic face of New Haven. Rather, these policies are intended to provide strength to existing areas of weakness, to more fully exploit the city's existing comparative advantages, and to accommodate market forces that from the perspective of local policy makers are largely outside their area of influence. The pursuit of this set of policies could be consonant with the economic and jurisdictional limitations confronting local policy makers and could ultimately benefit the city in jobs, tax dollars, and generally improved economic vitality. An economic development effort, however, is unlikely to be swift enough or to have a large enough effect to be a solution to the city's fiscal problems.

Chapter 3

Tax Exemption and the Local Property Tax

Robert A. Leone
John R. Meyer

When one speaks of local taxes in the United States, one is effectively speaking of the property tax. Recent years have seen the growth of other forms of local taxation, including sales and income taxes, but the property tax is still the dominant source of local government revenue in this country.[1]

Since America's early colonial period, particular properties have enjoyed exemption from property taxation. These properties generally belong to various "public service" institutions such as universities, churches, hospitals, governments, and others. Increasingly, proposals are being made to remove these tax exemptions as a means of solving local fiscal problems. In an effort to explore the wisdom of such proposals, this chapter provides quantitative estimates of the impact of tax exemption as applied in one medium-sized city, New Haven, and goes on to outline some policy conclusions that might be derived from the analysis.

THE BUDGETARY IMPACT OF TAX-EXEMPT PROPERTIES ON HOST MUNICIPALITIES: A CASE STUDY OF YALE AND NEW HAVEN

In the first chapter of this book it was argued that the central city can well expect increases in the numbers and importance of tax "immune" activities. It is not obvious, however, that the expansion of tax-exempt institutions is a "bad" turn of events for any particular jurisdiction. The fact is that many tax-exempt institutions do provide services that would otherwise be provided publicly and financed through taxation. It becomes important, then, to quantify more precisely the net fiscal effects—costs and benefits—of tax-exempt institutions. Here we are concerned primarily with quantifying the fiscal effects of a moderately expanding university (Yale) on a small city (New Haven). The emphasis throughout is the quantitative evaluation of the possible *net* budgetary impact of Yale on the city of New Haven.

In many respects, New Haven is quite typical of other small- to medium-sized cities which host nonprofit, tax-exempt properties.[2] Although the locally popular perception is that the tax-exempt "problem" in New Haven is Yale, it is essential to point out that Yale is only part of whatever such "problem" there may be. According to the *Quadrennial Reports on Tax-Exempt Property* of the State of Connecticut, in 1970 the city of New Haven had 44¢ in exempt property for every dollar of taxable property, a level more or less in line with national central city averages for such figures. Moreover, assessment figures on tax-exempt properties are not always accurate. Tax-exempt institutions rarely contest assessed valuations, even if these are obviously excessive, since they know that they will not have to pay the taxes. On the other hand, governments often have the right (as the state government does in Connecticut) to assess their own properties, and for political reasons these values may be systematically understated.

Table 3-1, which indicates levels of tax exemption in New Haven, highlights two facts. First, although universities dominate the New Haven exempt list, governments, at one level or another, account for a nontrivial 38 percent[a] of all exempt property.[b] Government facilities are immune (exempt) from property taxation presumably because if government were taxed, government would merely be taxing itself. This is not strictly true, however, since the level of government foregoing revenue is not always the level receiving the immunity. The fact is sometimes recognized and has resulted in various state and federal impaction formulas for payments in lieu of taxes.[c]

[a]From Table 3-1: Federal property (0.9%), State property (8.4%), City property (24.3%) and Housing Authorities (4.8%), for a total of 38.2%.

[b]This is, of course, a low figure, because highways, etc., do not enter any of the tabulations. When discussing tax exemption, it is also well to point out that there are degrees of exemption. Single family dwellings, for example, are in many cities uniformly assessed at effective rates lower than those which apply to multiunit dwellings. This is a form of exemption as is the usually token assessment of vacant land. These "exemptions" are above and beyond other mandated exemptions for the elderly, veterans, etc., none of which are shown in Table 3-1.

[c]Federal educational assistance for defense-impacted areas is one such program. At the state level, Connecticut has a PILOT (payment in lieu of taxes) program providing relief to cities and towns with heavy concentrations of state institutions.

Table 3-1.   Tax-Exempt Property in New Haven, 1970

1970 Gross Grand List (all taxable and exempt property)	$904,641,000
1970 Net Grand List (taxable property only)	$628,960,000
Percent tax exempt	30.5

Major Exempt Properties

	Millions of Dollars	*Percent of Total*
Federal property	2.5	0.9
State property	23.1	8.4
City	66.4	24.1
Private colleges and universities	103.1	37.4
Parochial and private schools	5.4	2.0
Churches	16.1	5.8
Hospital, veterans, and charitable organizations	31.8	11.6
Housing authorities	13.1	4.8
Other	13.9	5.0
	275.4	100.0

Source: Quadrennial Reports on Tax-Exempt Property, State of Connecticut, 1970.

A second point is not so well recognized, however. Government immunity from property taxation is understandable to the extent that the exemption is from that portion of the tax levied to pay for general social overhead expenditures. If, however, property tax immunity also means immunity from payment for specific, property-related services, then cost/benefit calculations for public investments will not adequately reflect the direct public service requirements of those investments. Just as tax-exempt status probably leads to property-extensive churches and universities, the immunity of government properties could lead to an oversupply of public capital facilities. In short, calculations of a hypothetical user tax bill could be useful for government-owned property. Although no net revenues to local government would result from the collection of these fees on its own properties, appeal to such a user tax bill might result in greater efficiency in public resource allocation.

The discussion that follows is limited to those budget and tax rate effects that are the direct consequence of tax-exempt status. No attempt is made to measure the aggregate economic impact of exempt institutions,[3] nor do we find such exercises especially productive. Our reservations stem from two sources. First, measuring the aggregate economic impact of any single major institution on a city is far from straightforward. For the most part, attempts to do so are demand oriented and ignore fundamental structural changes on the supply side of an urban economy. In order to identify supply effects, it is necessary to specify the alternative use of a piece of tax-exempt property. This is at best highly speculative. Second, from a policy viewpoint, these speculations are not likely to be very useful. Since we are interested in developing viable policy responses to given circumstances, it seems most reasonable to us to accept Yale's presence in New Haven and not speculate either on Yale's relocation or the nature of New Haven had Yale never existed.

In the early 1970s, for example, Yale University employed about 8,000 persons and spent about $135 million per year, but the impact of this employment and these expenditures on the city's revenues and expenditures had little to do with the tax-free status of the University. Of course, this is not strictly true. If taxed, Yale would probably be constrained to hire fewer workers and, over time, would probably use less property to produce its services. Similarly, tax-exempt institutions have a different job mix, they do not behave in the same way as profit-maximizing firms, and they might be expected to have different local effects for these reasons. These are, however, second order considerations.

Analysis

Our analysis is comprised of the following tasks: (1) calculation of a hypothetical property tax bill for Yale University on the premise that all taxpayers of the same status are taxed at the same rate; (2) calculation of a hypothetical "user-charge" bill for the university;[d] and (3) estimation of the level of public and quasi-public services provided to the community by the university.

We should stress that in the calculation of a hypothetical "user-charge" bill for the university we value all public services the university receives at cost; we have made no attempt to value services on a "willingness to pay" criterion. It is, of course, common practice for governments to levy charges at cost and not on a value of service basis. In addition, when valuing Yale-provided public services we use a similar cost basis. It is important to note that New Haven might provide Yale with services that cost as much as those that the university provides the city, but either institution may be getting a "better deal" than the other on a *value* of service basis.

dIn 1972 the Connecticut Tax Reform Commission recommended the levying of such charges on tax-exempt properties, and then Governor Meskill introduced the enabling legislation. Similar tax policies have also been popular in many urban renewal undertakings. Perhaps more important, given political fragmentation and the attendant capacity for individuals to escape general tax levies, the imposition of user charges may be a very attractive alternative to higher levels of property taxation.

The University As A Consumer Of Local Public Services

In estimating Yale's net burden on New Haven, the first step was to classify the city-provided goods and services into two basic categories: (1) those *direct* services for which a user charge could be identified and might be appropriate, and (2) those more "public" goods or *indirect* services that are paid by the "excise" on land use. (These categories were discussed in more detail in the first chapter of this book.) Generally, if the specific consumer of the service could be reasonably well identified, the service was classified as direct. Rubbish removal was perhaps the most obvious example. Sewerage, street lighting, street maintenance, and fire and police protection were also placed in this category (but with rather more difficulty). It would have been desirable to have subdivided indirect services into social overhead items and administrative overhead for the direct services identified. We did not do this, although, in principle, cost accounting methods might permit it, at least to a first approximation.

The Markup Procedure

As a second step toward calculating a hypothetical total property tax bill for the university (sufficient to pay for both services received and a "fair" share of the excise burden), we adopted a direct cost markup allocation principle. That is, we defined the share of the social and administrative overhead allocable to a user of municipal services to be some multiple, or markup, of its direct service costs. In the simplest case, this markup could be calculated as the ratio of total municipal government expenditures to direct expenditures for the entire community. If, for example, a city had a $40 million budget of which $10 million was identifiable as direct services, the markup would be $40 million divided by $10 million, or 4. For every $1 of direct services consumed, a user would be taxed $4 in order to pay both its direct costs plus a share of the social and indirect overhead.

An alternative to the markup, of course, would be the estimation of the hypothetical tax bill by taking the city's assessment of the value of tax-exempt property and applying the existing tax rate (adjusted for the lower rate that would apply if exempt property were taxed). This obvious and standard alternative was not used for three reasons. First, unlike taxed property holders, there was no cause for either the city or the exempt institution to be concerned about the accuracy of assessments of tax-exempt properties. Second, many exempt properties (usually government-owned) declared their own assessed valuation, often without provision for appeal by the taxing authority or constituency.[e] Third, the very concept of fair market value—the usual basis for assessment in the private sector—was ambiguous when applied to many exempt facilities. (For example, what was the "market value" of Yale's Sterling or Beinecke Libraries or the local federal court house?)

The markup approach, in addition to circumventing many of these assessment problems,[f] had one other distinct advantage. Where markups are calculated for individual classes of municipal service users, it becomes clear that certain types of property finance a larger share than others of indirect and overhead municipal costs. A higher markup for industrial property than for residential property is a widely accepted fact and accounts for efforts by cities to attract industry in order to alleviate fiscal problems. Higher markups, of course, are also an incentive for those so taxed to relocate.

To calculate markups for various types of properties we first divided all property in New Haven into four categories: industrial, commercial, residential, and public properties. Markups were calculated for the first three categories while the direct services consumed by public properties (e.g., fire protection provided to City Hall) were classified as indirect municipal expense. In determining the level of direct municipal services allocable to the university, it was necessary to classify Yale's tax-exempt properties into these four categories. Hence, Yale's laboratory facilities were classified as industrial property, office space as commercial property, and dormitories as residential.

Certain university holdings were also classified as public properties and the direct services allocable to them were *not* assigned to the university. Of Yale's 170 structures, four seemed to be essentially public facilities: Harkness Tower (which is a public monument bell tower); Beinecke Rare Books Library (which has periodic special displays of rare books and related artifacts and is a major tourist attraction in New Haven); the Peabody Museum of Natural History; and the Yale Art Gallery. Services allocable to the non-Yale educational functions of these buildings were classified as public on the grounds that these are essentially facilities operated by the university for the benefit of the public (i.e., non-Yale-related people). Counts of actual

---

[e]In the New Haven case this meant, for example, that Southern Connecticut State College, constructed at a cost of at least $41 million, would be assessed for approximately $25 million at the going assessment rates, were it not allowed to declare its own valuation of $12 million.

[f]However, to the extent that the consumption of some services such as fire protection is a function of property valuation, some of the problem remains.

use of the above facilities tended to confirm this presumption. A benefit allocable to the "esthetics" of the bell tower seemed more difficult to establish.

A fair portion of the university's physical plant is also devoted to federally funded research. Two different approaches to evaluating the direct services allocable to these properties were considered. In one set of calculations those local public services provided to federally occupied properties were excluded from Yale's allocation on the grounds that the tax exemption on these properties is a pass-through from the local to the federal government and not to the university. In a second set of calculations these services were assigned to the university.

After determining the property classes, we then calculated the property tax revenue associated with each class. Using procedures described in detail in the Appendix to this chapter, we next assigned all the costs of direct services to property classes. Given the tax revenues attributable to a property class, we calculated the markup simply by dividing the total tax bill by the direct service allocation :

Markup for a given property type =

$$\frac{\text{Total property tax revenue associated with that property type}}{\text{Total cost of direct services allocated to that property type}}$$

In New Haven, residential property bears a decidedly lower markup on direct services than either commerical or industrial property. Alternatively, one could say that a higher percentage of the tax on residential property pays for services directly attributable to residential property. For instance, residential property owners in New Haven in 1971–72 paid $2.94 in taxes for every dollar of direct services they consumed, industrial property paid $4.65, while commercial property paid $5.67 for every dollar of directly allocable services. A more sophisticated markup procedure than that mentioned above would be to estimate the hypothetical property tax bill by applying separate markups to residential, industrial, and commercial properties held by the tax-exempts.

The level of any markup also depends on the breadth of the tax base included. In particular, horizontal equity or neutrality principles would suggest that all nonpublic tax-exempt property should be treated the same. Accordingly, when estimating Yale's hypothetical tax bill, markups were employed that would apply if Yale and all other tax-exempt properties in New Haven paid taxes. As previously noted, commercial properties in New Haven currently pay $5.67 in property taxes for each dollar of direct services consumed. However, if all exempt property were taxed, the markup for commercial property could be lowered to $4.74 without lowering the total revenue from commercial properties.

The Findings

Table 3-2 summarizes the calculations. The findings are quite striking. Total services consumed by the university represent slightly over 1 percent of the city's total budget and less than 6 percent of the cost to the city of all identifiable direct services. Yale constitutes approximately 37 percent of noncity-owned exempt property; thus if Yale is typical of tax-exempt institutions, total revenues from all currently exempt property at full taxation would be $7.8 million. This is approximately the same as the tax increase in New Haven in a recent fiscal year.

This finding suggests that if local revenue collections from tax-exempts were limited to financing *direct costs* the loss of tax-exempt status for universities and others probably would not be especially burdensome. City direct services consumed by Yale constitute only about 6/10 of 1 percent of Yale's annual operating budget. One suspects that the problem of tax-exempt status for universities would be essentially a "nonissue" were it not for the social markup (the "excise" portion of the property tax). Including the markup, Yale's assessment for city-incurred expenses runs at about 2 percent of Yale's annual budget.

The University As A Source Of Public Services

The university, like most nonprofit institutions, is a major supplier of public services as well as a consumer of those services. Whether these university services are of "full" value to the local citizenry is debatable. For example, one might presume that most college and university towns have more museums and libraries than the citizenry would otherwise freely choose. On the other hand, cities and communities probably provide universities with some services that are deemed of little value by the university.

Table 3-3 summarizes estimates of services provided by Yale that might be deemed substitutes for public expenditures. The benefits of these expenditures have been allocated to state or to local government depending upon which one would likely be responsible for providing the service in the absence of provision by the university. On this basis, for example, the annual cost of post-secondary educational programs and mental health programs, substitutes for public services

Table 3-2. Direct Services to the Tax-Exempt Property of Yale University, by Property Class, and Yale's Hypothetical Tax Bill (000's of dollars), 1971-1972

Direct Services	Classes of Yale University's Tax Exempt Properties[a]			
	Commercial in Nature	Industrial in Nature	Residential in Nature	Total
Police	$ 38.7	$ 6.0	$ 95.4	$140.0
Fire	223.7	97.8	240.5	562.0
Sewers	8.7	17.6	19.8	46.1
Streets	7.1	2.4	29.3	38.8
Lights	4.5	1.5	26.2	32.3
Total Direct Services	$282.7	$125.3	$411.2	$819.2 (Line A)
Assumption I[b]				
Markup	3.34	3.34	3.34	3.34 (Line B)
Hypothetical property tax (Line A × Line B)	$944.1	$418.6	$1,373.5	$2,736.2
Assumption II[b]				
Markup	4.74	3.52	2.67	3.51 (Line C)
Hypothetical property tax (Line A × Line C)	$1,339.9	$441.1	$1,097.9	$2,878.9

[a]Excluding costs of services to federally occupied properties and properties classified as public.

[b]Assumption I is that the markup for Yale is equivalent to what the average markup for the City would be if all property were taxed, while Assumption II allows the markup to vary by property class (again assuming all property is placed on the tax rolls).

Source: See Appendix 3-A.

Table 3–3. Net Costs to the University for Public Service Programs, 1971

	Governmental Jurisdiction Benefiting from Yale-Provided Service		
	City of New Haven	State of Connecticut	Persons Served[a]
	(000s)	(000s)	
Yale College		$ 732	488[b]
Graduate School		291	194
School of Medicine		608	86
Law School		123	45
Yale Art Gallery	$ 540		124,000[c]
Peabody Museum	618		262,000[d]
Libraries:			
Law		41	Not Available
Medicine		52	NA
Architecture		14	
Kline Science		26	
Reference		17	
Hill Health Center	264*		5,000
Connecticut Mental Health Center		852*	3,700[e]
Child Study Center		110	2,750
Upward Bound	23*		75
New Haven Institutes of Allied Health Careers	12		47
Hill Dwight Day Care Center	30		40
Yale Council of Community Affairs	76		NA
C. Hill Day Care Center	15		27
Education Improvement Center	15		150
Community Advocate for the Conn. Mental Health Center	30	14	200
Total	$1,623	$2,880	

*University support is the forgiveness of indirect cost recoveries on outside grants and contracts which directly support the program.

[a]Unless otherwise noted, refers to number of persons served in the governmental jurisdiction benefiting from the Yale-provided service.

[b]Includes approximately 100 residents of the City of New Haven.

[c]Includes over 6,650 New Haven public school children.

[d]Includes over 15,000 New Haven public school children.

[e]Includes almost 2,000 residents of New Haven.

often provided by state governments, is approximately $2,880,000. The total cost to the university for those services "benefiting" the city is $1,623,000. The total cost for all university-rendered public services is $4,503,000.

Comparing Table 3-3 with Table 3-2, the existing pattern of tax exemption assumes a certain crude justification. Yale does provide public services with a total cost in excess of any seemingly defensible tax assessment that might be placed on the university. It could certainly be argued that in Yale's absence the city would not necessarily provide all the services Yale currently provides; nevertheless, at a minimum, it seems highly probable that if Yale were not in the community, the city of New Haven would have to spend a good deal more than it now does on health, education, and day care services.

In summary, these benefit calculations clearly indicate that the conventional defense for at least this one university's tax-exempt status has some merit. And, we suspect that the Yale case is not atypical. The calculations also suggest, however, that state government, and not city government, is the prime beneficiary. Again, we would be surprised if this were not the usual case, given the character of most universities' services and involvements. This supports the recent Connecticut Tax Reform Commission, which recommended, in essence, that the state compensate local municipalities for the foregone markup on tax-exempt properties; however, the Commission also recommended that the tax-exempt institutions themselves pay their own direct service costs, a policy that may or may not follow depending on how and whether the university is compensated for the public services it provides the local community.

SUMMARY AND CONCLUSIONS

Approximately one-third of the nation's real property is currently exempt from local property taxation.[4] Economic considerations indicate that if effective property tax rates continue to increase and to remain highly differentiated between central cities and their suburbs, then the eventual market solution will be for central cities to house a disproportionate share of those tax-exempt properties. Whatever the cause, central cities feel increasingly burdened by the presence of exempt properties in their midst. Economists would suggest that the solution to the problem might be to analyze the legitimacy and appropriateness of the property tax. After all, unusually heavy excise taxes on a particular good tends either to inhibit consumption of that good or to induce its "bootlegging." The "bootleg alternative" is clearly rather difficult with real estate excises (though special tax reductions for new construction or urban renewal in some central cities may be a partial substitute). Flight from the city becomes the usual circumvention.

The ultimate financial effect of urban decentralization, from whatever cause, is the well known fiscal crisis that confronts many central city mayors today: the demand for urban public services goes up as the means to pay goes down. There is no easily identifiable solution to this problem, at least as long as cities remain within the confines of the property tax. To expand revenues from the property tax, either the tax base has to be expanded (i.e., more property values added to the rolls) or the tax rate on the existing base increased. The latter is not a popular remedy, and it may be self-defeating to raise existing central city tax rates much further. As matters stand, these rates may often capture virtually all the capital appreciation in real estate values so that higher effective rates could lead to an actual decrease in wealth held in real property and, in the process, could seriously distort real investment decisions as well. Moreover, to increase property tax revenues through tax base expansion is almost certainly less painful than increasing revenues through higher taxes.

One possible way to expand the tax base is, of course, through economic growth (see Chapter Two). Unfortunately, few central cities have this option, especially in the industrially mature area of the northeast. Most of these cities are so fully developed that there is not room for much economic growth—and besides, growing suburban markets, labor supply areas, and transportation facilities make suburban locations otherwise attractive.

It is quite understandable, then, why there has been considerable discussion of the alternative of increasing the tax base by eliminating existing exemptions. To place this policy alternative in better perspective, this case study documents the quantitative *net* budgetary impact of one major tax-exempt institution on a host municipality. Our focus has been on the net impact, because tax-exempt institutions normally do render services that are public in character. The usual defense for tax exemption of nonprofit institutions is, in fact, that they provide services that otherwise might be provided only through taxation.

But even without consideration of what tax-exempts do for their host municipalities, removing tax exemption for private nonprofit institutions apparently would not greatly affect the fiscal positions of most central cities. The sums involved are simply too small. Indeed, if the imposition of taxes would induce the tax-free institutions to withdraw those public services that they now render, the net effect of taxing presently exempt properties might be to worsen, not to improve, the fiscal plight of central cities. Furthermore, if, after the removal of tax exemptions in a central city, local property tax rates were still higher than in surrounding jurisdictions, tax-exempts could be expected to make some of the same adaptations that the private sector is making—namely, withdrawal from central sites and less use of land. Of course, tax-exempts might do this more slowly than their private counterparts, being less subject to competitive pressures. Nevertheless, the basic incentives could well be the same. In short, the unfortunate truth may be that "beggaring thy neighbor" is rather inappropriate when one's supply of neighbors is already in jeopardy!

Appendix 3-A

The Calculations of Direct Costs

This appendix[a] contains a general description of the techniques used to estimate the direct municipal services costs reported in Table 3-2. It is difficult to estimate the sensitivity of our estimates to our assumptions. Where possible, we have indicated the direction of possible bias. We have no reason to believe, however, that any serious distortions exist, or that slightly different assumptions will lead to substantially different estimates. (A possible exception, described in detail below, is the fire service allocation.)

The determination of what services are and are not directly allocable is somewhat arbitrary. It is almost universally agreed, for example, that primary education has sufficient spillovers for the public at large, as well as the individual student, to benefit significantly. It is not so obvious that the same can be said for public parks and recreational facilities or for street lighting. It is worth noting that in the case of education (if directly allocated), the added costs to universities and other tax-exempt properties would be virtually zero in most cases, since public school students rarely reside in current exempt university housing. If education were allocable, markups would fall, as would the university's hypothetical property tax bill.

The following sections of this appendix present the assumptions and calculations for the components of directly allocable services,

[a]This appendix is a summary of a description of calculations prepared by Stephen Silberman and Elisa Nash Miller, published in "Report of the Joint Study Group of the Legal and Economic Relationships Between Universities and Their Host Municipalities," Yale University, August 9, 1972, Section IV. All tables in the Appendix are derived from this report.

namely, fire protection, police services, sewerage, streets, lighting, and parks and recreation.

Fire

This entire budget item (except for a fireboat, but inclusive of pensions and debt service) was considered a direct service (Table 3A-1).

The cost of fire protection is conceptually one of the most difficult of municipal services to allocate by land use. Initially, an attempt was made to estimate the probabilities of fire occurring on different classes of property. These efforts were eventually abandoned when it became clear that the data were inadequate for determining expected losses with any reasonable degree of accuracy.

The alternative selected was to allocate fire services according to the value of fire-vulnerable property (property that can be damaged by fire) without any adjustment being made for the probability of fire occurring. The value of fire-vulnerable property was calculated by subtracting the value of land from the city's tax accounts and adding estimates of untaxed furniture and fixtures. The totals of fire-vulnerable property are found in Table 3A-2.

It is not clear what bias, if any, is introduced by ignoring the incidence of fires by property type. To the extent that Yale's property may be overvalued, the fire protection service provided the university is exaggerated. However, if the expected loss to the university property were high (due either to a high incidence of fires or heavy damage in the event of fire) then inflated property values would be offset.

To check the reasonableness of the estimate of fire services used by the university, we investigated three universities that provide their own fire protection without relying on outside help. Table 3A-3 summarizes data for Stanford University, Purdue University, and the University of Illinois. Stanford University's fire department serves not only the campus proper but also 600 family residences leased near campus. Moreover, Stanford has 6,000 acres of grass and woods and an extremely dry summer climate, which together present a

Table 3A-1.   Firefighting Budget

Total 1971–72 operating budget (less fireboat)	$4,585,000
Pensions	716,000
Debt	116,000
	$5,417,000

Table 3A-2. Fire-Vulnerable Property, by Land Use (000's of dollars), 1970

Residential Property	
Taxable structures	$149,840
Contents	37,460
Outbuildings	4,959
Housing authorities	12,697
	$204,956
Commercial Property	
Structures net of land	$117,747
Merchants inventories	32,278
Furniture and fixtures	16,751
Other	16,980
	$183,756
Industrial Property	
Structures net of land	$ 24,730
Manufacturers inventories	27,968
Machinery	36,467
Furniture and fixtures	3,431
Mechanical tools	1,369
Utility items	13,380
Other	3,478
	$110,823
Yale Property	
Structures net of land	$ 89,294
Furniture and fixtures	22,324
Other	145,205
	$256,823

substantial fire hazard unlike any at Yale. The large grassland area, the extremely dry climate, and the numerous residences on campus all seem to indicate that this figure would be a high estimate of Yale's fire protection costs.

Our estimate of the cost of fire protection delivered by the city to Yale University is also high in comparison to the costs at Purdue University and the University of Illinois where costs range from $200,000 to $500,000. Although our fire service cost estimate of $802,000 is high relative to the service for these other universities, it probably reflects an extremely effective level of service provided by New Haven to the university. Yale is surrounded by four fire stations, which undoubtedly provide greater protection than the university would choose to have if it were supplying its own protection.

Table 3A-3. Summary Information for Three Universities Supplying Their Own Fire Protection

	Stanford	Purdue	University of Illinois
Full time firemen	46 (work 56 hr/wk) plus 14 student firemen	18 (work 56 hr/wk)	36 to 39 (work 56 hr/wk)
Major pieces of equipment	9 (plus several smaller pumps)	3 (plus 1 car)	4 (plus 1 car)
Operating budget	$535,000—main campus station $265,000—accelerator substation	$212,000.	$444,600. (confidential)
Capital budget	—	Less than $10,000/year.	$10,000/year
Runs per year	—	370	250
Mutual aid (1971)	Given—6 Received—2	Given—2 Received—1	Given—6 to 8 Received—2
Population served	25,000	Over 25,000	Over 35,000
Area served	8,000 acres 2.1 million sq.ft. of academic buildings	—	12 million gross sq.ft.
Assessed value	—	—	$1 billion (replacement); $450 million (original cost)
Insured value	—	Over $370 million (buildings & contents)	—
Number of buildings	160 to 170 major	140	500, 200 major
High rises	6 buildings to 12 stories; others 5 or less	Several 12 stories; many 8 stories	4 or 5 of 12 stories; average 4½

Police

The total budget of the city of New Haven for police service, exclusive of pensions and debt service, was $5,481,000. Initially, this budget item was divided into two categories: overhead and nonoverhead expenditures. Nonoverhead expenditures were then further subdivided into allocable and nonallocable activities. For example, the activities of the gambling and narcotics division and those of the traffic and license division were not considered divisible by different land use, while those of the patrol division were (see Table 3A-4). In short, some police services are labeled direct and others indirect. Since 82.3 percent of total nonoverhead expenditures were for direct services, 82.3 percent of overhead expenditures were also considered directly allocable. The final step was to add to these direct service costs the appropriate proportion of pension payments and annual debt payments, bringing the total direct services for police protection to $5,481,000.

The method used to distribute these direct service expenditures among the various land uses was based on discussions with police department officials, who observed that time and resources spent on patrolling (the largest police activity), and the planning of patrol routes, were highly correlated with the number of crimes reported in an area. Moreover, the investigation of crimes by the detective division, as well as the activity of the communications division, are likewise highly correlated with reported crimes. Thus, even though some patrol activity involves responding to calls which are not crime related (minor accidents, nuisance, etc.), all direct services were allocated on the basis of reported *criminal* activity.

The allocation procedure was extremely simple and straightforward in concept. The police department has available a map which identifies the number of crimes reported on each 600-square-foot

Table 3A-4. **Allocation of Police Expenses (000's of dollars)**

Pure Overhead	
Administration	
Planning and budgeting	
Support services	
Records and data processing	
Training and personnel	$1,011
Direct, Nonoverhead Services	
Communications	
Detective division	
Patrol	3,680
Indirect, Nonoverhead Services	
Intelligence	
Gambling and narcotics	
Traffic and license	
Youth service	790
Total	$5,481

plot of land within the city. This mapping of reported crimes was superimposed over a land use map so that it was possible to count the number of reported crimes committed on commercial, industrial, residential, Yale, and "other" property. Direct police services were then allocated among the various land uses in the same proportion as reported criminal activity. The results are shown in Table 3A–5.

The simplicity of this approach does introduce some probable errors, but there is no evident systematic bias against any individual land use category. One immediately apparent distortion is the implicit assumption that the services provided to investigate and protect against each type of crime are equal. However, there are many different types of crimes, and it was not believed that the accuracy gained by assessing these individually would justify the expense.

An additional methodological difficulty involves the "spillover" effects between the Yale and New Haven police forces. Yale police are available to help the city should such a request be made, and the city police do book and hold persons arrested by the Yale police even if the city police are not involved in the arrest. Moreover, the city annually spends an average of $7,000 training Yale's police force. For want of any adequate way to quantify the net effect of these spill-ins and spill-outs, we have assumed they cancel one another.

Sewerage

A common method used to allocate the cost of sewers and sewage treatment among different land users is to assume that sewerage is directly proportional to water use and to apportion the cost accordingly: an industrial plant which consumed, say, one-twentieth of the municipal water supply would be charged with one-twentieth of the cost of sewage treatment and sewer installation and maintenance. This approach has four principal weaknesses. First, it is not true that water used and sewage created are perfectly correlated. Much of the

Table 3A–5. **Distribution of Police Expenses, by Property Class**

Type of Property	Number of Crimes	Percent Share of Direct Police Services
Commercial	9,641	24.2
Industrial	2,063	5.2
Residential	25,120	62.8
Yale	1,254	3.1
Other	1,872	4.7

water consumed by households, for example, is used to water lawns and never enters any sewage treatment plant.

Second, it may be considerably more expensive to treat the sewage originating from an industrial plant than that originating from residential sources. Third, the cost of installing and maintaining sewer facilities depends not only upon volume of sewage handled, but also upon the density of users. In residential areas, for example, considerably more feet of pipe may be needed to handle a given quantity of sewage than would be needed in downtown areas. In downtown areas, however, maintenance costs may be higher since the space under stress is used much more intensively.

Finally, water use data are often inadequate. For example, the New Haven Water Company does not even report water consumption by the city of New Haven. Instead, it records the water consumed by the entire metropolitan area. However, the composition of users differs in suburban areas, where residential users constitute a higher proportion relative to industrial and commercial users. In addition, there are some industries that supply their own water from wells or other sources, but dump their effluent into the municipal sewers. These considerations suggest that the share of water supplied by the New Haven Water Company to industrial users in the New Haven *metropolitan area* is only weakly correlated to the share of water supplied to industry within New Haven proper.

Attempts were made to correct for some of these deficiences. However, we were forced to assume that the ratio of industrial to commercial and residential water use was the same throughout the entire New Haven metropolitan area, an assumption likely to underestimate the share of sewerage costs that ought to be allocated to industrial and commercial land users in New Haven proper. Using figures from the New Haven Water Company on the percentages of water supplied to the metropolitan area by property type, sewerage costs were allocated under the assumption that all water used by public, industrial, and commercial users was returned to the municipal sewers, and that all water used by residential users (except that used for sprinkling) was also returned to the municipal sewers.

This procedure is likely to overestimate industrial sewage for two reasons. First, some water used by industries is incorporated into their product; and second, other water is treated by the industrial plant itself and then returned to one of New Haven's rivers rather than to a municipal sewer. Offsetting these biases, which tend to overestimate industrial sewerage costs, is a third bias: industrial wastes cost more to treat. The net effect of these biases is unclear; we were forced to assume that they cancel one another. With regard to Yale there is likely to be an upward bias, if any. Although it was assumed that all of Yale's water is returned to the sewers, some is used for watering, and some is lost through evaporation in the university's heating plant.

The figures for commercial sewerage costs reported in Table 3A-6 include nonprofit institutions other than Yale. In our analysis we have usually allocated these costs along with public properties under the general category "other." For consistency it was necessary to make some assumptions and to adjust these figures. From previous analysis we know that the value of services provided to other institutions, excluding the city, has been approximately one-half the value of services provided to Yale. Yale's sewerage was 4.6 percent of the total, so we considered that 2 percent of sewerage services should be subtracted from Commercial and added to the Public item to make a total of 6.1 percent for other tax-exempt properties. This reduces the Commercial figure to 13.0 percent (see Table 3A-6). The cost of the sewerage system is shown in Table 3A-7.

Streets

The entire streets and highways budget, $785,000, was considered allocable by property use. Activities included in this budget item are:

Fall leaf cleaning
Sand barrels services
Spring cleaning
Snow
Bulk refuse
Street paving
Hurricane cleanup
Regular street cleaning program

One approach considered was to divide the city by commercial, industrial, residential, Yale, and "other" street frontage, and to allocate costs to the various land uses in the same proportion as frontage is allocated to the five land uses. However, for certain items—particularly street cleaning, street paving, snow, and hurricane cleanup—more time and resources are spent in the central business district and its surrounding areas than in the outermost parts of the city. Alternatively, more time is spent in the outer residential areas than in the downtown area on such items as fall leaf cleaning (since there are fewer trees downtown), and on sand barrels (since only salt is used downtown). Our problem, then, was how to weight these distinct areas when distributing costs.

One weighting system readily available was that which treated the

Table 3A-6. Allocation of Sewerage Expenses to Property Type

Sewerage Usage by Property Type		
	(1) Millions of Gallons	*(2)* Percent of total
Residential Sewerage[a] (total water consumed net of sprinkling)	8,636	41.8
Industrial Sewerage[b]	7,143	34.5
Public Sewerage	851	4.1*
Yale Sewerage (no water netted out for sprinkling)	957	4.6
Commercial Sewerage[c]	3,099	15.0*
Total	20,686	100.0

*In allocating sewerage expenses, the 4.1 percent figure for Public Sewerage was raised to 6.1% and the Commercial Sewerage figure lowered correspondingly to 13%. This shift, described in the text, is to account for the fact that some nonprofit institutions are included in the 15 percent figure.

[a]Domestic water consumption was calculated as follows:
(1) It was assumed that each resident uses 60 gallons per day.**
(2) There were 394,344 residents in the area served by the New Haven Water Company in 1970.
(3) $394,344 \times 60 \times 365 = 8,636,134,000$.

[b]The New Haven Water Company supplied 5,221 million gallons to its industrial users. From data collected in 1960 it was determined that industrial water users in New Haven drew approximately 73 percent of their water supply from the municipal system, the remainder coming from wells and rivers. Multiplying 5,221 million by 1.368 yields 7,142 million for the total gallons used by industry in the area served by the New Haven Water Company.

[c]Commercial sewerage was calculated by subtracting from the 14,758 million gallons consumed by commercial *plus* residential users.
(1) 8,636 million gallons used by households for domestic purposes.
(2) 2,066 million gallons used by households for sprinkling.
 Howe and Linaweaver found the average eastern dwelling unit used 185 gallons per day during the summer for sprinkling. There were 124,108 occupied dwelling units in 1970 in the area served by the New Haven Water Company.

**See Charles W. Howe and F.P. Linaweaver, Jr., "The Impact of Price on Residential Water Demand and Its Relation to System Design and Price Structure," *Water Resources Research* 3 (1): 13-32.

Table 3A-7. Cost of Sewerage System

Sewers and drains	$ 728,000
Bond debt	975,000
Cost	$1,703,000
Less fees	39,000
Net	$1,664,000

central business district as most important, the concentric circle surrounding it as next in importance, and the other portions of the city as least important. This is in fact how street cleaning activities are allocated, and it was felt that this could be used as a weight for other activities in the various districts of the city. Using this system for allocating the entire list tends to overestimate the cost of services to commercial and Yale properties, because leaf removal and sanding (where more time is spent on residential property) are important cost items. However, since street paving, snow removal, and cleaning are also major items, this does not appear to be too great a distortion.

The method used was to superimpose the 18 street cleaning districts of the Public Works Department over a land use map to estimate street frontage by property type in each district. Then, applying the weights used in street cleaning to each district, and summing the relative time spent on each type of property in each district, we estimated the distribution of this budget item for the five types of property. Results are shown in Table 3A-8.

Lights

The city's bill for street lights was $766,000. The intensity (and therefore the cost) of lighting depends upon land use and traffic flows. Small residential streets are illuminated with lights of low intensity; heavily populated residential or commercial areas are illuminated with much brighter lights. To determine the distribution of services to different land users, a map of all the street lights in the city of New Haven was superimposed over a city land use map. Then the number of street lights of each intensity bordering commercial, industrial, residential, Yale and other property, was determined. The cost of service allocable to each land use was found by multiplying the number of lights of each intensity by the annual rate charged for each light and then summing all intensities (Table 3A-9).

Parks And Recreation

The total operating budget for parks and recreational services net of fees was $1,194,734. As in the case of police services, some of these activities were considered allocable, while others were considered nonallocable (Table 3A-10). Parks and squares, trees and horticulture were considered nonallocable because the amenities which they provide are enjoyed by citizens whether they are working or relaxing, and whether or not they are residents of New Haven. Senior centers were viewed as similar to education or public health services —a responsibility of the community at large, and thus treated as nonallocable.

Table 3A–8. Percent of Total Time Spent on Street Maintenance Activities, by Property Use

	Percent
Commercial property	16.3
Industrial property	7.4
Residential property	64.7
Yale tax-exempt property	6.7
Other tax-exempt property	4.9

Table 3A-9. Percentage of Total Value of Street Lighting Services Attributable to Property Type

Property Type	*Percentage of Total Value of Street Lighting Services*
Commercial	11.9
Industrial	5.4
Residential	73.8
Yale	5.7
Other	3.2

Table 3A-10. Total Operating Budget for Parks and Recreational Services, Allocable and Nonallocable

Nonallocable	
Parks and squares	$528,917
Tree division	104,455
Horticulture	52,012
Senior centers	80,802
Total	$766,186
Allocable to Residential Property	
Recreation division	$315,131
Lighthouse Point	35,744
Golf course	64,475
Skating rinks	42,193
Swimming pools	26,932
Edgewood Park	49,242
Gross total	$533,717
Less fees	−105,169
Net total	$428,548
Grand total	$1,194,734

The golf course, skating rinks, and swimming pools can easily be considered allocable simply because fees are charged for their use. Moreover, these activities, like those of the recreation division, are used by people in their role as residents and not as workers. Similarly, Lighthouse Point and Edgewood Park, because of their location, are enjoyed by residents primarily in their leisure hours, and so are also allocated to residential property.

This division is admittedly an arbitrary one. It could be argued that all recreational activities, like educational services, ought to be financed by the community at large. However, since there are fewer ostensible benefits to the entire community from recreational than from educational expenditures, the former are more often financed by levying charges against the immediate user. Hence, it is a matter of judgment whether or not these services of the parks and recreation division should be considered allocable. Since 60 percent of nonoverhead expenditures are nonallocable, 60 percent of the $87,407 of administrative costs for these services are also considered nonallocable. (The totals are shown in Table 3A–11.)

Allocating Services To Yale University

In our judgment it would be improper to allocate services to each type of property at Yale by taking the total bill for a particular service and dividing it according to the proportion of Yale's assessed property in each land use category. (See Table 3A–12.) That is, if 28 percent of Yale's property is commercial, it does not follow that 28 percent of the cost of police services should be allocated to commercial property at Yale. Our objection is based on the observation that $1.00 of commercial property is not provided the same amount of, say, police protection as $1.00 of industrial property.

Thus we proceeded by first calculating the value of each direct municipal service per dollar of commercial, industrial, and residential property in the city at large. These calculations showed that on the average a dollar of commercial property in the city received $.55 of police protection, while one dollar of industrial property received $.25, and residential property $1.12 of police protection. For sewers, the corresponding figures were $.09, $.54, and $.17; for fire they were $.56, $.72, and $.49. Fire services per dollar of property differ because of different ratios of fire-vulnerable to invulnerable property for each land use category.

The next step was then to multiply these values by the amount of Yale property in each land use category and use the resulting figures as weights by which to allocate each direct service provided Yale.

Table 3A-11. Final Allocation of Total Budget for Parks and Recreational Services

Indirect services	$818,000
Direct services (to residential property)	$464,000

Table 3A-12. Breakdown of Yale Property (In Terms of Assessed Value) According to Land Use (000's of dollars)

Property	Amount
Commercial	$28,504
Industrial	9,684
Residential	34,677
Federal industrial	14,730
City commercial	12,043

Table 3A-13. Assignment of Public Services Allocated to Yale, by Property Type

Property		Percent of Total
Yale commercial	.0055 × 28,504,000 = 156,772	23.4
Yale industrial	.0025 × 9,684,000 = 24,210	3.6
Yale residential	.0112 × 34,677,000 = 388,382	57.7
Federal industrial	.0025 × 14,730,000 = 36,825	5.5
City commercial	.0055 × 12,043,000 = 66,237	9.8

Again using police as an example, we have the calculations shown in Table 3A-13. Yale commercial property is thus allocated 23.4 percent of the police services provided to the university. Yale industrial property receives 3.6 percent, Yale residential property 57.7 percent, while federal industrial property at Yale receives 5.5 percent, and, finally, city commercial property at Yale receives 9.8 percent of total services.

✳ *Chapter 4*

Municipal Income Taxation

Christopher H. Gadsden
Roger W. Schmenner

As noted at several points in preceding chapters, the pillar of public finance in America's cities and towns has long been the property tax. Indeed, in many parts of the country, the property tax remains the sole source of locally generated tax revenue. Recently, however, a number of cities and towns have reduced their dependence on the property tax by tapping an additional source of local revenue, income.

A key question to many, then, is whether the substitution of a municipal income tax for a property tax is "good policy". Deciding this issue means comparing the economic and legal implications of local property and income taxation. To this end, this chapter describes the municipal income tax (section I), contrasts its nature against that of the property tax (section II), and then examines the economic arguments for and against each (section III). Later sections survey the various legal constraints on a city's authority to tax income (section IV), and contrast the municipal income tax with other more indirect policies (section V). Finally, the chapter explores whether the city of New Haven could impose an income tax on its own initiative, and indicates its likely effects (section VI).

I—BRIEF HISTORY OF THE MUNICIPAL INCOME TAX

Although Charleston, South Carolina reportedly taxed income prior to the Civil War, the oldest local income tax still in effect was enacted in 1939 by the city of Philadelphia. The Philadelphia tax—essentially a flat percentage levy against the earned income both of residents and of nonresident workers—has become a frequently copied model. In 1946, Toledo, Ohio followed Philadelphia's lead, and was in turn followed by Louisville, St Louis, and hundreds of municipalities throughout Pennsylvania and Ohio. By 1970, more than 3,500 local jurisdictions in nine states were levying some form of local income tax, although 3,458 of those jurisdictions were doing so within the borders of Ohio and Pennsylvania.

Although the income tax is now employed by municipalities of all sizes, it was originally implemented to relieve the projected revenue shortfalls of some larger cities. Each major city which adopted the local income tax did so because it was faced with huge budgetary deficits.[1] The point is an important one. The income tax was not initially adopted because cities thought it was in some sense a "fairer" tax than the property tax, but solely because it was a tax that could generate large amounts of revenue.[a] The revenue generating capabilities of the municipal income tax, while important, are not its only merits. The income tax offers other advantages when compared to the property tax. Before making such a comparison, however, the natures of the two locally levied taxes should be carefully described.

II—DESCRIBING THE PROPERTY AND MUNICIPAL INCOME TAXES

For many cities, the property tax is really two distinct taxes. All cities tax real property—land, improvements to that land, and structures on that land. Not all cities tax personal property, however. Personal property can be of two types:

1. Tangible personal property, which includes vehicles, commodities, livestock, and furniture. Towns in Connecticut do generally tax personal property, although on average it accounts for only about 10–15 percent of their tax bases.[2] Of this amount, automotive vehicles, boats, inventories, machinery, and office furniture are most important.

2. Intangible personal property, which consists of money, bank deposits, stocks, bonds, mortgages, and other assets. Such property is particularly difficult to trace and for that reason it has become more and more prone to exemption from taxation. Connecticut's towns do not tax intangible property.

[a]A possible exception is Baltimore. The local income tax applies to Maryland's 23 counties as well as to Baltimore itself. Baltimore's tax was not adopted unilaterally by that city but was rather legislated by the state.

The property tax can be characterized, then, as a tax on land and capital, both physical capital and, in some states, financial capital.

The nature of the municipal income tax differs radically from the property tax. In its simplest form, the tax is a levy on the wages of residents no matter where they work and on the wages of workers who commute to the taxing jurisdiction. This is the "Philadelphia model" of the income tax. In many instances, however, the tax base is augmented to include the earnings of both incorporated and unincorporated business.[b] Thus, while the property tax can be seen as a tax on land and capital, the municipal income tax can be seen for the most part as a tax on labor income and business profits.

Double Taxation

This distinction between local property and income taxes points to a number of complexities inherent in the income tax. Unlike real property itself, workers are free to move around and they need not live in the same jurisdiction in which they work.[c] Such freedom of movement and location leads to some ambiguity as to who pays how much income tax to whom. Consider two towns situated side-by-side only one of which taxes income. Under a typical municipal income tax statute, residents of the town which levies the tax as well as those who only work in the tax-levying town must pay the tax. People who both live and work in the nontax levying town are the only ones to escape paying the tax.

Suppose that the one town decides to join the other in levying a municipal income tax. Everybody will now pay an income tax, but it is not clear who will pay which town. Do commuters between the towns pay both taxes, one of which is levied against them as residents and the other levied against them as commuting, nonresident workers? This question of double taxation is a real one and one that has been debated extensively throughout the history of the local income tax.

With the exception of Philadelphia, it has been decided by legislatures and courts of law that commuters are not to be subject to double taxation. Double taxation is avoided in a number of ways. Three are mentioned now, with a fuller legal discussion found in section IV. Double taxation is avoided when: (1) the jurisdiction of

[b]Business earnings are generally defined according to IRS conventions although there are some slight modifications, notably in Missouri. Pennsylvania is conspicuous in prohibiting its municipalities from taxing business earnings.

[c]Of course, tangible personal property can move around. There is always a fair amount of litigation as to the situs in any given year of industrial and commercial inventories for purposes of local personal property taxation. Also, computers are often placed where there are low rates of personal property taxation.

residence claims its full tax levy; (2) the jurisdiction of employment claims its full tax levy; and (3) the jurisdictions split the tax levy, usually on a 50–50 basis.

In all cases of possible double taxation, where the tax rates differ between the towns, the established convention to avoid double taxation (e.g., (1) or (2) above) is followed. The affected commuter, however, is liable for the maximum single town tax bill. For example, in Pennsylvania, the convention is for the jurisdiction of residence to claim its entire tax levy from any commuters. If the town of employment imposes a higher tax rate than the jurisdiction of residence, it is then entitled to the excess tax collected.

Suburbs are sometimes irate when central cities begin taxing the incomes of their residents. The convention adopted to treat the issue of double taxation can often act as a stimulus for the spread of income taxation to suburban jurisdictions. If by levying an income tax these suburban towns can deny commuter revenue to the central city, they often act promptly to pass a municipal income tax. For this reason it is quite commonplace for large cities in Pennsylvania and Ohio to be surrounded by suburbs which also tax income, frequently at the same rate as the larger, central city. Within a year after the imposition of an income tax in Cleveland, 45 of the surrounding suburbs also taxed income. Around Pittsburgh, almost all of the suburbs tax income, often sharing the returns with local school districts.

Apportioning Business Income Subject To Tax

In cases where business earnings are also taxed, business concerns with operations in two or more jurisdictions are subject to an ambiguity not unlike that associated with the commuter. It is deemed unfair for the business operation located in an income tax levying town to pay its tax on the net earnings from all its multilocation activities; some apportionment of net earnings should be made among the jurisdictions in which the business is located. This problem has been recognized and conventions have been adopted to deal with it.

The most common means of apportioning business earnings among jurisdictions is the so-called Massachusetts formula. Under this scheme the percentage of business earnings attributable to operations in a particular municipality can be computed as the average of three ratios: (1) the ratio of payroll paid from operations in the municipality to the total payroll from all business locations; (2) the ratio of gross receipts in the municipality to total gross receipts; and (3) the ratio of total real and personal property located in the municipality to the total business property found in all locations.[d]

Other Issues

The municipal income tax base need not confine itself to earned income (wages and salaries) and business earnings (corporate earnings or net receipts of unincorporated business). Other types of income may also be applicable: rentals, dividends, and capital gains. As it happens, the vagaries of state law often dictate what type of income can or cannot be taxed. The taxation of earned income and business earnings is nearly universal, but only in Maryland, Michigan, and New York City is general unearned income taxed. Ohio permits the taxation of rental income, as part of business income, but other types of unearned income are not taxed.

With an income tax, the question of proportionality versus progressivity is often raised. Progressivity can be affected either by graduated rates or by exemptions. Most municipal income taxes are levied at flat percentage rates with no exemptions. However, Maryland, Wilmington, and New York City have all offered graduated rates of one kind or another. The Maryland counties and New York offer a sliding scale up a number of income ranges. Prior to amendment Wilmington's was most abrupt with marginal tax rates at the cut off points in excess of 1500 percent of additional income. Both New York and Wilmington permit exemptions. A more complete discussion of the legal aspects of this issue are discussed later, in section IV.

Diversity in the Municipal
Income Tax

With such a wealth of ambiguities and complexities to be confronted and resolved in order to legislate a municipal income tax, there is considerable variation in the "income taxes" employed across jurisdictions; in part these differences arose from the diverse paths followed by municipalities in order to assess such a tax.

Philadelphia and New York went as mendicants to their respective legislatures and pleaded for the necessary enabling legislation. Toledo and Detroit on the other hand, completely ignored their state legislatures. Instead, they enacted income tax ordinances on

[d]In Michigan the business can also choose any one of the three ratios (payroll, sales, or capital) as the appropriate percentage.

their own and convinced their state courts that they had proceeded legally.[e] Louisville, Kentucky lacked the legal authority to tax personal income but capitalized on its delegated power "to impose and collect license fees on . . . franchises, trades, occupations, and professions."[3] In 1948 Louisville enacted an Occupation License Tax on the privilege of engaging in any business, occupation, calling, profession, or labor within the city limits. The measure of the license fees was conveniently set at 1 percent of any wages, salaries, or receipts. Kentucky courts have steadfastly upheld a distinction between a true income tax and this "license fee" despite a Federal ruling that it was a distinction without a difference. Gadsden, Alabama has also succeeded in adopting an Occupational Privilege Tax which is tied to wages and salaries earned in the city.

The inherent ambiguities of the tax and the convolutions of state law have combined to give great diversity to the kinds of municipal income taxes in existence. Table 4-1 summarizes this diversity for some major cities.

III—EVALUATING THE PROPERTY AND INCOME TAXES

Before the local income tax can be analyzed in terms of the standard criteria of vertical and horizontal equity, economic efficiency, location incentives, or administrative cost, and then compared to the property tax, we need to address the question of tax incidence—i.e., who bears the real, as opposed to the nominal, burden of a tax.

Tax Incidence

Historically, the issues of property tax incidence[4] has been divided into two: the incidence of the tax on the land itself, and the incidence of the tax on the reproducible and movable capital situated on that land. It is generally acknowledged that the incidence of the land tax depends primarily on the supply characteristics of land. If land is fixed in supply, the land tax is clearly borne by landowners. Insofar as land is variable in supply, the tax burden may be shifted to users of land, the extent of the shift depending on the price elasticities of both the supply of and the demand for land. The indeterminancy is instructive. The incidence of a simple land tax, rather than being completely straightforward, turns out to be fairly ambiguous and fundamentally dependent on two elasticities, the values of which are often difficult to estimate precisely.

[e]A later section of this chapter (IV) deals explicitly with the variety of legal problems and issues raised by the municipal income tax.

Table 4-1. Comparative Table of Local Income Taxes in Ten Major Cities as of 7/1/73

	Baltimore	Cincinnati	Cleveland	Detroit	Louisville	New York	Pittsburgh	Philadelphia	St. Louis	Wilmington
First year of tax	1967	1954	1967	1962	1948	1966	1954	1939	1948	1969
Tax earned income?	yes	yes	yes	yes	yes	yes	yes	yes	yes	yes
Tax unearned income?	yes	no	no	yes	no	yes	no	no	no	no
Tax corporate income?	no	yes	yes	yes	no	no	no	yes	yes	no
Tax non-resident commuter?	no	yes	yes	yes	yes	yes	yes	yes	yes	yes
Do suburbs tax income?	counties	some	yes	yes	county	no	yes	no	no	no
Tax credit or sharing	no n/a	yes against town of residence	75% to town of employment	50% to town of employment	credit against county tax	no	yes against town of employment	no	no	no
Rate structure	graduated of state	2.0%	flat 1%	flat 2%	flat 1.25% plus .75% for Schools	graduated 0.7-3.5%	1.0%	flat 3 5/16%	flat 1.0%	flat 1.5%
Allow exemptions?	yes	no	no	yes	no	yes	no	no	yes	no
Who collects tax?	state	city	intercity coll. agency	city	city	city	city	city	city	city
Administrative cost for property tax[a]	1.14%	1.08%	0.62%	1.31%	1.44%	0.5%	1.20%	1.30%	1.01%	0.8%
Administrative cost for income tax[a]	0.65%	1.4%	0.78%	1.66%	0.76%	2.0%	1.48%	0.93%	2.22%	0.6%

Sources for this table include: Md. Ann. Code Art. 81 283 (1975); Ohio Rev. Code Ann. 718.01 et seq. (Supp. 1972); Mich. Comp. Laws 141.501 et seq. (1967); Ky. Rev. Stat. 91.260 (1971); New York General City Law 25-a et seq. (McKenney 1968); Pa. Stat. tit. 53 15971 et seq. (Supp. 1972); Mo. Stat. Ann. 92.110 et. seq. (1971); Del. Code Ann. tit. 22901 et seq. (Supp. 1970); Advisory Commission on Intergovernmental Relations, "The Commuter and the Municipal Income Tax," M-51 (April 1970).
[a] As percent of revenues collected by tax.

The incidence of a tax on capital is much more complicated and ambiguous than that of a land tax. Mieszkowski has analyzed the issue in two parts: the incidence of the base portion of the tax, common to all taxing districts; and the incidence of tax differentials, which vary across taxing districts.[5] Mieszkowski argues that the base portion of the property tax, assuming perfect mobility of factors, perfect markets, and no effect of taxes on savings behavior, is very much like a profits tax and thus is likely to be borne by the owners of capital. The argument treats the value of capital as the net present value of the stream of returns to that capital, so that taxing the returns affects the value and taxing the value affects the returns.

A uniform tax on capital will lower the rate of return to that capital, and if capital is perfectly mobile and markets are perfectly competitive, the rate of return to all capital is reduced. However, to the extent that all capital is not perfectly mobile, that all markets are not perfectly competitive, or that savings may be sensitive to the tax rate, the burden of a uniform property tax ceases to be strictly on all owners of capital. If the capital stock is adjusted because of altered savings behavior, other factors may suffer a smaller return. If capital is not mobile, all owners of capital will not bear an equal burden. If perfect competition does not prevail, owners of capital may be able to shift the tax forward to consumers or backward onto labor. It is easily seen, then, that the incidence of a uniform and universal property tax is far from clear.

When attention turns to the incidence of tax differentials between jurisdictions, the issue becomes even more complex and ambiguous. A blizzard of assumptions is required in order to trace out the theoretical incidence of the tax. Suffice it to say that, in general, the burden of tax differentials is greater for landowners the more elastic the supply of labor and capital, the more elastic the demand for the output, the stiffer area-wide competition, the lower the elasticities of substitution of land for other factors of production, and the more meager the returns to the land from alternative uses. To the extent that these assumptions fail to apply, the more likely the shifting of tax burdens will be. Similar considerations are pertinent to an investigation of the incidence of the municipal income tax. Numerous assumptions have to be made before the tax burden can be theoretically assigned to landowners, users of land, capitalists, consumers, or labor.[f]

[f]Unique among municipalities, San Francisco levies a "Payroll Expense Tax" against *employers*, assessed at 1 percent of total payroll. (San Francisco Ord. No. 275-70, as amended by No. 378-73.) The question looms whether its incidence is any different from a tax on employee wages.

The issue of tax incidence for both the property and municipal income taxes is further clouded by the distinction between short run and long run tax incidence. The degree of real tax burden is likely to be heavier in the short run than it is in the longer run. If factors are mobile and the tax capable of being shifted, taxpayers over time may be able to distribute themselves geographically over a metropolitan area so as best to avoid the tax. Activities immune to high tax rates, or nearly so, will not hesitate over time either to stay or to locate in higher tax areas; activities particularly sensitive to high tax rates will more likely locate over time in the lowest tax rate areas.

The point to be made by this brief and incomplete excursion is that tax incidence is an exceedingly complex issue, hardly to be resolved by a priori reasoning. Our empirical knowledge is scant and thus we can say little with any real confidence about actual tax incidence. This ignorance has a very real bearing on how surely and effectively we can compare the property and local income taxes.

Vertical Equity

Despite the possible consequences of the incidence arguments above, it is widely alleged that the property tax is regressive—i.e., that it takes away a higher percentage of the income of poor people than it does of richer people.[g] Assuming that no income class is more adept at shifting an income tax away from itself than any other class, the typical municipal income tax may also be very mildly regressive.

That it is regressive at all can be attributed largely to its typically being a tax on earned income only and not on unearned income. Very high income families derive a lower fraction of their total income from wages and salaries than do low and middle income families and thus a municipal payroll-only tax would be a less burdensome type of income tax for these high income families. However, it should be recognized that family income must reach $25,000 before the earned income/total income fraction dips very much below the level that prevails for poorer people. Evidence on this point is documented in Table 4-2.

Moreover, the income tax has the advantage of being readily adaptable for eliminating regressivity, either by including all types of income into the tax base or by adopting differential tax rates. Some

[g]The truth of this statement depends in principle upon the income elasticity of demand for housing as well as the relative magnitude of the excise component of the property tax. In addition, it is alleged that the administration of the tax systematically underestimates the value of expensive properties. The empirical evidence on these points is mixed. See the section on the property tax in the American Economic Association's *Papers and Proceedings* (May 1974), pp.212-235.

Table 4-2. Wages as Percent of Adjusted Gross Income, by Income Class, North Atlantic Region

Income Class	Wages as % of Income	Income Class	Wages as % of Income
Total	.808	$ 9,000–10,000	.895
No adjusted gross income	.743	10,000–15,000	.914
<600	1.013	15,000–20,000	.877
600–1,000	.905	20,000–25,000	.803
1,000–2,000	.793	25,000–30,000	.707
2,000–3,000	.757	30,000–50,000	.595
3,000–4,000	.790	50,000–100,000	.454
4,000–5,000	.828	100,000–200,000	.335
5,000–6,000	.877	200,000–500,000	.189
6,000–7,000	.868	500,000–1,000,000	.095
7,000–8,000	.885	>1,000,000	.043
8,000–9,000	.900		

Source: U.S. Internal Revenue Service, Statistics of Income 1969 Individual Income Tax Returns. Washington, D.C.: U.S. GPO, 1971.

caution should be observed, however, before dogmatically asserting the superiority of the municipal income tax. While it is likely that the municipal income tax is less regressive than the property tax, in the long run, taxed parties may be able to locate so as to reduce their tax burdens to the point where there is no significant difference between the burdens of the property and income taxes. Nevertheless, no matter what the true incidence of both income and property taxes may be, it is at least apparent that the incidence of the income tax can be altered systematically by legislating tax base and rate changes more easily than the incidence (and thus the vertical equity) of the property tax can be.

Horizontal Equity

The property tax is also notorious for horizontal inequities brought by assessment procedures. Assessments are seldom regular and only infrequently do assessments in different locations imply the same ratio of assessed to market value. Moreover, it is widely alleged that higher valued structures and dwellings are relatively underassessed. The proposed remedy—assessment reform—is often discussed, but in practice is costly and difficult to effect. In contrast, under an income tax, provided that all forms of income are treated alike, equals are treated equally as a matter of course. To the extent that all forms of income are not placed into the tax base, then some horizontal inequity may surface. Nevertheless, the problems of horizontal inequity are probably reduced under an income tax.

Uneveness in liability is even more of a horizontal inequity problem for the property tax than is unevenness in 'assessment.[6] Ever since the origins of the property tax, certain kinds of properties have been exempt from taxation. In many cities, over one-quarter of the total assessed value in the city goes tax free. In New Haven, almost one-third of the property pays no tax. Moreover, tax exemption appears to be growing, especially in central cities. Under an income tax the problems of tax exemption evaporate. Employees of tax-exempt institutions must pay a municipal income tax, be they federal, state, or local government employees, college professors, or clergymen. If some employee tax liability gets shifted backward, then tax-exempt institutions will bear a portion of the local tax burden themselves.

There are also some substantial differences in the abilities of the local property and income taxes to treat equals equally over time. Between property reassessments, many horizontal inequities in the property tax may actually widen since some persons' ability to pay may change relative to other persons. The income tax will be less susceptible to such changes over time.

Economic Efficiency and Location Incentives

Two other tax evaluation criteria—economic efficiency and location incentives—are both extremely difficult to judge either theoretically or empirically. They rest to a great degree on tax incidence.

Consider economic efficiency, the matching of resources to their most productive uses. In general, efficiency can be said to be disrupted by non-neutral taxes. If the property tax could be considered simply as an excise on housing services, it would be clear that the property tax would be less economically efficient than the income tax, needlessly diverting resources away from the housing sector. Unfortunately, homeowners can legitimately be viewed as investing in housing as well as consuming it, and this makes the analysis much more complex. In this view the property tax, rather than being solely an excise, is a tax on income from capital as well; and as such it must be compared to taxes like the corporation income tax. If one also considers the personal income tax advantages from home owning, then the property tax, as a tax on income from capital, compares favorably with other such taxes, thus spurring home ownership and the consumption of housing.

On balance, it is difficult to assess precisely whether property taxation implies an allocation of resources away from or toward the housing sector. Traditional thought has advocated the former view, while much recent thinking has supported the latter.[7] In any event, the property tax is not likely to be neutral in its effect on housing consumption. Income taxation, however, is much more likely to be neutral in its effect and thus arguably better than the property tax in terms of economic efficiency.

Tax incidence also has a direct bearing on location incentives. The greater the tax burden borne by a household or firm itself, the greater is the incentive for that household or firm to seek a new location where its tax burden will be less. If, as theory suggests, the income tax (a tax on both payrolls and business earnings) is probably borne more fully by firms than a property tax, then we should expect that the location incentives set in motion by income tax rate differentials are greater than those set in motion by property tax rate differentials. This expectation has been somewhat confirmed in a study of manufacturing locations.[8] Locational incentives thus argue against the municipal income tax, all other things equal, but the argument is not a strong one. The evidence is simply too weak to be heavily relied on.

The vast revenue generating capabilities of the municipal income tax may also work to the disadvantage of small jurisdictions. The smaller a political unit becomes, the greater the chance it lacks a diversified economic base—in the extreme, "the company town." Reliance upon an income tax in such a jurisdiction intimately links tax revenues to the business fortunes of the local industry. If tax rates remain constant, economic declines which trigger worker layoffs or significant drops in business earnings subject to tax may bring a drastic reduction in tax flows.[9]

Administrative Cost

Another possible disadvantage of the municipal income tax is the cost of its administration and collection. Unless economies of scale in administration and collection are reaped, the municipal income tax is more expensive to levy than a property tax of equal yield. Furthermore, since no municipality to date has proposed the total abandonment of the real property tax in favor of income taxation, the costs of income tax administration have to be added to the existing costs of property tax administration.

In small communities the costs of income tax collection and enforcement may amount to 10 percent or more of the revenue yield.[10] This figure does not include the expense and aggravation imposed upon local employers who withhold up to 70 to 80 percent of the tax from wages and salaries. In regions where many jurisdictions impose a separate income tax, the withholding burden on the employer can be considerable.[11]

Through economies of scale, larger cities have been able to reduce the percentage of revenue taken up by collection costs. In Detroit, for example, direct costs amount to 2.2 percent of the revenue yield, and total costs, including an allocable share of overhead, amount to 3.2 percent.[12] The Maryland system has the collection made by the state along with the state income tax, with revenues passed back to the counties. Such large scale operations are definitely to be preferred. Table 4-1 provides a comparison of property and income tax collection costs for ten major cities. More discussion of tax collection costs follows in section V.

Summary

In sum, the municipal income tax is a possible substitute for the local property tax. It is probably a more equitable tax both within an income class and across income classes, and it is certainly more readily adaptable to yield desired changes to taxpayer equity. It is likely also to be more economically efficient. Further, given a centralizing of administration, the collection costs of a municipal income tax can lie below that of the property tax (see Table 4-1). Only for location decisions is there a reasonable presumption that the income tax has adverse consequences, and even there the evidence is as yet too weak to be conclusive.

IV—LEGAL AUTHORITY TO TAX INCOME

The city council of a municipality may not be entirely free to enact whichever type of local income tax will maximize tax revenues. State constitutional provisions, statutes, or the decisional law of the state courts may sharply curtail the authority of some cities to raise revenues from an income tax.

As a starting point, the legal constraints can be divided into two categories: (1) those threshhold barriers that might negate the power of the municipality to tax income at all; and (2) those state law doctrines that restrict the type of permissible income tax. It will be seen later that the categories are in fact artificial, for the legal constraints define a continuum of municipal authorizations to tax various elements of income.

Threshhold Barriers

The legal obstacles to initial passage of a local income tax take three forms. The first, and most difficult to surmount, is a state constitutional prohibition against an income tax by municipalities. Two states—Florida and Tennessee—have strictures in their constitutions against such a levy. A second barrier may be a state statute forbidding local income taxes. Six states—Alaska, Kansas, North Carolina, South Dakota, Virginia, and Wisconsin—specifically ban the taxing of income by towns, cities, and counties.[13]

A third and different form of restriction arises from the application of Dillon's Rule. In his treatise *Municipal Corporations*, Judge Dillon stated the rule as follows:

> . . . it is the general and undisputed proposition of law that a municipal corporation possesses, and can exercise, the following powers, and no other: First, those granted in *express words*; second, those *necessarily* or *fairly implied* or *incident* to the powers expressly granted; those *essential* to the declared objects and purposes of the corporation.[14]

The Rule limits the authority exercisable by city governments.[15]

The doctrine of preemption, which springs from the same legal proposition as Dillon's Rule, forms a link between the first category of total bans against income taxation and the second group of legal constraints, which restrict the type of tax. It has been applied in various jurisdictions to serve both functions. In essence this doctrine provides that municipalities are subordinated to the state and given narrowly circumscribed powers. In the area of taxation, preemption precludes municipalities from assessing any class of subjects or objects that the state government taxes. Preemption may be explicitly set forth by statute[16] or developed in decisional law by a state judiciary.[17] The doctrine places the city at the mercy of the state's financial needs and desires.

Legal Constraints on the Type of Income Tax

The second category of legal constraints comprises restrictions on the nature of income tax that municipalities may levy. These restrictions operate upon two major characteristics of the tax—the tax base and the rate structure. The preemption doctrine, discussed above as a threshold barrier, plays a major role in limiting the type of permissible tax.

Tax Base. A local income tax could be viewed as a package of different levies on income—a tax on payroll, another tax on rents, a third on capital gains, and so forth. Thus one municipality could elect to impose one of the taxes without accepting the entire package. In other cases individual levies in the package might be invalidated judicially while others survive. In the ensuing paragraphs the barriers to a broad-based income tax are studied through examination of the legal issues raised with each major element of income.

Wages and Salaries. The lowest common denominator of local income taxation is the so-called payroll tax assessed against gross earnings. The payroll levy is placed on all earned income of residents of the jurisdiction; all income taxing jurisdictions, except the Maryland counties, also levy upon the income earned within the jurisdiction by nonresidents.

Nonresidents who must pay this "commuter income tax" have raised numerous complaints and challenges. The first is that they face double taxation, for in the most common case the commuter pays a wage tax to the central city where he works and a property tax and/or a second wage tax to support services in his suburban residence. At least one state court dismissed this complaint summarily on the ground that the commuter derived benefits from both communities. But such an answer is insensitive to a genuine taxpayer predicament, for the commuter derives full benefits from neither community, yet he or she pays more taxes than resident employees in either town. On the other hand, the commuter arguably receives more total benefits than resident/workers in either town and should pay more than a single measure of tax. Unquestionably an attempt to quantify the benefits in either or both towns would prove to be a monumental undertaking, but the outcry of "double taxation" has not fallen on deaf ears. Sympathetic state legislatures have mitigated the effect of the "double tax" through a variety of practices.[h]

In a second legal challenge, nonresidents have alleged that taxation of their wages violates rights of due process. They question whether the city of their employment has jurisdiction to impose a tax upon them.[18] Commonly, jurisdiction to tax a person is founded upon residence,[i] and commuters have claimed that they are deprived of a political voice in the setting of the tax. However, the rationale for a wage tax upon nonresidents is a benefits principle. The commuter has availed himself of the privilege of conducting business in the city and has received municipal protection and services during his working hours. In return the city measures the benefits received by the income generated within its boundaries and charges accordingly.

While most commuters would concede that they do receive some benefit from services provided by the city of employment, they would

[h]See section II, above.
[i]The typical direct tax is the capitation tax or head tax, which is assessed at a flat rate against each resident individual in the jurisdiction.

argue as a third legal challenge that no effort has been made to determine the extent of the benefits.[19] However the prevailing test for income taxes, which the U.S. Supreme Court announced in *Wisconsin v. J. C. Penney*,[20] imposes a fairly low standard. Under this test, taxation of nonresidents need only bear "some fiscal relation to the protections, opportunities, and benefits" afforded by the municipality. State courts have consistently ruled that this charge-benefit relationship has been reached.[21]

Rents, Dividends, and Capital Gains. Unearned elements of a potential income tax base have not withstood legal challenges as successfully as the payroll tax. For varying reasons local taxes in Pennsylvania, Delaware, Missouri, Kentucky and Alabama reach only worker earnings and possibly the net profits of local businesses. Since this type of tax base restriction reduces the potential revenue yield[j] and tends to make the impact of the tax more regressive,[22] the reasons for sheltering unearned income from municipal income taxes are significant and instructive.

One source of income derives from rentals of real and tangible personal property. In several states, however, the inclusion of rental income in the local income tax base is proscribed by a uniformity clause in the state constitution. Such a clause typically requires that state or local taxes fall evenly upon classes of persons or property.[23] An income tax on rent is often regarded as a tax on the underlying property.[k] This conclusion stems from the observation that the market value of property is a capitalization of all future rents and enjoyments to be derived from the property.

The attribution of taxes on rents to the underlying land was a fundamental part of the famed *Pollock v. Farmers Loan & Trust Co.* decision,[24] which found a nineteenth century federal income tax unconstitutional. While that decision was reversed by the Sixteenth Amendment to the United States Constitution, the theory that property values are a capitalization of rents and enjoyments remains basically sound. The income tax reduces net rentals and hence the capitalized value of the rental stream, so that it becomes indistinguishable from a direct tax upon the property.

jThis result occurs because certain forms of income are sheltered from taxation. The tax reaches only wages and salaries which typically account for roughly three quarters of the adjusted gross income.

kIf this principle is accepted, one might hypothesize that a sales tax is a tax on the goods being transferred, as is an inheritance tax. In each case the tax is levied upon one incident of ownership. Only a tax on personal services eludes possible categorization as a property tax.

Where real or personal property is subject to a local property tax, rented property would be subject to two taxes—an income levy and the property tax—while the owner-occupied property faced but a single tax. Thus taxation would not be spread evenly across this class of property, and the uniformity clause would be offended.[1] The Supreme Court of Pennsylvania has excluded rents from the local income tax base, partly on uniformity grounds.[25] Dividends and capital gains have been excluded from the income tax base in Pennsylvania (indeed, in all municipal income taxing states except Maryland, Michigan, and New York) for the same reason.[26]

Corporate and Unincorporated Business Association Income. Cities in Alabama, Michigan, Missouri, and Ohio are permitted to tax the net profits of corporations doing business there. With respect to corporations, the benefit principle, and not residency, is the prevailing rationale for municipal income taxation. Thus the city has jurisdiction only to tax profits (or gross receipts, in the case of Alabama) that are earned within its limits. Clearly, a great number of companies conduct business in more than one municipality necessitating methods of apportioning their profits among localities.

Several allocative schemes are presently employed. One method is the use of separate books and records to reflect what work was done in each taxing jurisdiction. Most municipalities taxing income approve of this scheme.[27] For some operations, however, segregated bookkeeping might become very cumbersome. For that reason most of the states permitting local taxation of corporate income authorize an averaging scheme called the "Massachusetts" or "St. Louis system,"[28] which was discussed above in section II. Most cities that currently tax income impose a levy on the net profits of unincorporated business associations as well. Partners who both reside and work in the city are taxed fully, whereas nonresident partners are taxed according to the share of their income earned within the city.[29]

Rate Structure. State law may also dictate the rate structure for municipal income taxes. Commonly, the enabling legislation imposes a ceiling on the tax rate.[30] Such a limit is consistent

---

[1]If the uniformity clause is construed to mean the net tax burden to the individual (and not the number of taxes for which the individual is liable), then it should be noted that the individual may not suffer any more from the imposition of two taxes than from the imposition of just one. Depending on the workings of the market, the net burdens of the two tax systems may be the same. Of course, a real burden standard would not be a feasible one for the court to adopt; economists are far from agreement on tax incidence.

with the administration of a property tax for which many states impose an upper limit on millage. But with income taxation there is an additional variable in the rate structure, for the taxing jurisdiction can choose between graduated and proportionate (flat) rates. In most states that now permit local income taxation, however, only a flat rate is required. Flat rates are prevalent both because of cities' reluctance or insensitivity to considerations of vertical equity[31] but also because progressive taxation has been legally banned in some states.

In Pennsylvania the judiciary has ruled that the state constitutional uniformity clause[32] requires proportionate taxation. Where graduated rates are permitted, considerable flexibility in rate structure is permitted. The Maryland counties and New York City impose similar taxes. An individual's first thousand dollars of taxable income in New York City is subject to a 0.7 percent rate, and after several intermediate graduations, all income over $30,000 is taxed at a 3.5 percent rate.[33]

Wilmington, Delaware also instituted graduated rates for its municipal user tax.[34] Instead of graduating the income ranges as New York does, however, it classified taxpayers by their total earned income. Thus, in class I, which embraced taxpayers earning less than $4,000 annually, no tax was charged. Taxpayers in class II, who earned between $4,001 and $6,000, paid ¼ percent of *all* earned income, not just the excess over $4,000. And taxpayers in class III, who earned more than $6,000, paid ½ percent of all earned income.

Some inequities did appear at the bounds of the classes. For example, a taxpayer making $6,000 per annum paid $15 tax. A taxpayer making $1 more ($6,001) paid $30.01 tax. The single dollar of earnings caused a $15.01 increase in tax—a marginal tax rate of 1501 percent! Not surprisingly, a taxpayer with an annual earned income just over $6,000 brought a class action suit on behalf of himself and taxpayers similarly situated to contest this rate structure. The Supreme Court of Delaware, however, found the rate structure in compliance with both the equal protection clause of the Fourteenth Amendment and the uniformity clause of the Delaware Constitution because the tax brackets represented genuine differences in economic well-being.[35]

A second vehicle for progressivity in a tax structure is the exemption. In Pennsylvania the judiciary has invalidated exemptions as a backdoor method of implementing graduated rates.[36] Other flat rate states, however, permit exemptions to shield certain minimum incomes from tax.[37] Commonly these are personal exemptions, flat allowances for each dependent plus the head of the household. Like the Internal Revenue Service, New York City grants additional exemptions for the aged and the blind.[38] New York has further instituted the so-called "vanishing exclusion," a modification of the exemption privilege that provides a lesser exemption for taxpayers in higher income brackets.[m] Such an exclusion amplifies the progression in effective tax rates.

V—MUNICIPAL INCOME TAXATION: VARIATIONS AND ALTERNATIVES

In this section we present several alternative approaches to taxation that have been or could be implemented with a view to retaining the desirable characteristics of the municipal income tax but minimizing three economic disadvantages which we previously identified: (1) the ease of factor relocation, (2) high administration costs, and (3) vulnerability of small jurisdictions to business declines.

Inter-municipal Cooperation

One empirical observation that has been made about the local income tax is that larger cities experience lower collection costs per revenue dollar than do smaller municipalities. It follows that neighboring cities which levy an income tax could profitably enter into cooperative arrangements to eliminate duplication of efforts. Such a cooperative venture could entail mere information sharing or involve a far more extensive approach.

One extensive effort along these lines has developed in metropolitan Cleveland. It was recounted earlier that some 45 towns in the greater Cleveland area responded to the Cleveland city income tax by enacting ones of their own. In 1968 some 34 towns entered into a compact entitled the Agreement for Central Collection of Municipal Income Tax.[39] Under the Agreement the Cleveland Central Collection Agency was created to administer the tax for participating cities. As part of the compact, steps were taken to effect uniform tax procedure in all cities—similar Boards of Tax Review in each city, common tax due dates, and uniform filing forms.[40]

An alternative to establishing a new agency is a contractual undertaking by one city to collect taxes for surrounding municipalities.

---

[m]Under the "vanishing exclusion" nonresident taxpayers with incomes of $10,000 or less may exclude (exempt) a maximum of $3,000 from their taxable income; taxpayers whose annual income lies between $10,000 and $20,000 are permitted to claim a maximum of $2,000; the $20,000-30,000 range has a $1,000 ceiling on exclusions; and no exemptions are allowed where adjusted gross income exceeds $30,000 (*N.Y. Gen. City Law* § 25-m sec. 2 (b) (McKinney 1968). This system magnifies the progression in effective tax rates considerably.

The School District of Williamsport, Pennsylvania, performs this function for its neighboring communities.[41] The collection expenses are allocated among the participating subdivisions according to the number of items processed.[42]

The Metropolitan Taxing District

Another variation for the municipal income tax is the metropolitan taxing district. One model for this, albeit not an income tax model, was the proposed Four County Metropolitan Capital Improvement District in metropolitan Denver.[43] The district, embracing the four counties surrounding Denver, was authorized to levy a sales and use tax in each county and return the proceeds (less ½ percent of the revenues for expenses) to the city or county in which they were collected. In effect, the district served only as a collection agent for the political subdivisions that comprised it.

Such a special district could be adapted to collect a local income tax. It would logically realize all the efficiencies and economies attributed to the joint administration schemes discussed under the previous heading, while vastly decreasing the opportunities for tax flight. Indeed, elimination of sales tax avoidance through relocation was the political impetus for the Capital Improvement District in Denver.[44]

State/Local Cooperation

The introduction of state participation increases the possibilities for a better municipal income tax. State assistance might range from a sharing of state expertise with local tax officials to actual collection of the tax on behalf of the cities. The costs and benefits to the municipality of each system must be separately considered. At one extreme the state could provide only technical assistance to the political subdivisions taxing income.[45] However, even greater administrative savings could be realized from a tax supplement. Under such a plan municipal units may elect to "piggyback" a local income tax on top of the state-assessed tax.

At present there have been but two examples of local piggybacking upon a state *income* tax. Counties in Maryland and the city of Baltimore piggyback on the Maryland state income tax. The rate, to be established by each local unit, is permitted to range between 20 and 50 percent of the state tax.[46] In 1968 Bernalillo County undertook a similar arrangement with the New Mexico state income tax.[47] Tax supplements have been more extensively adopted in the sales tax area where New York City and local units in California, Illinois, and Mississippi have imposed them.[48] The piggyback tax, when viewed as a form of local income tax, unfortunately is not now well suited to handle the commuter problem. The use of tax credits and tax sharing to avoid double taxation of the commuter requires segregation of income according to source. State tax returns do not now provide this information; they would have to be modified to do so.

The state's role can be expanded beyond mere administration. Several states have adopted a tax *sharing* scheme to eliminate income tax harbors within their boundaries. Under this arrangement the state imposes an income tax and distributes a portion of the proceeds to local units of government. Currently, for example, Wisconsin places approximately 40 percent of its income tax revenues in the shared revenue fund, which is apportioned to city, town, and county governments.[49] In effect every municipality in a tax sharing state imposes, by state fiat, a uniform income tax; the state tax commissioner serves as collection agent for this mandatory levy.

Tax sharing thus combines the efficiencies of a piggybacking approach with the uniformity of a state tax. Whether the problem of an undiversified economic base is mitigated depends upon the formula for allocating revenues to local governments. In Ohio, which adopted a tax sharing income levy in 1972, the language of the state constitution suggests that a municipality will receive 50 percent of what it would have collected from a local tax at the same rate.[50] That approach will not solve the problem. On the other hand, the funds could be apportioned on any systematic basis that served the political needs of the state. Per capita allocation to municipalities is one possibility; this model could even be adjusted for the income level of each city. To retain the commuter-contribution aspect of the local income tax, the apportionment formula could even incorporate employment statistics.

Federal/Local or Federal/State/Local Cooperation

Logically another variant of the municipal income tax would incorporate the federal government. Federal revenue sharing is an obvious extension of state tax sharing and will not be discussed further. However, the unparalleled economies of administration and collection realized by the federal Internal Revenue Service are worthy of some additional mention.

At present the Internal Revenue Service does not collect income taxes levied by state or local governments. Several states do piggyback, however, in the sense that their income tax is measured as a percentage of the taxpayer's federal tax liability.[51] These tax supplement statutes have presented several problems. First, the piggyback statute commonly incorporates a prospective conformity provision which adopts as state law both present federal definitions such as net income and adjusted gross income and any future amendments to the federal Internal Revenue Code.[52] The legal objection to this provision is that it represents an improper delegation of state law-making authority to the federal government. In *Cheney v. St. Louis Southwestern Ry.* the Arkansas Supreme Court adjudged such a statute unconstitutional.[53] Other state courts, however, have taken a more practical view, recognizing that the state legislature has not relinquished its power to repeal the conformity statute.[54] The need for uniformity seemingly outweighs this arguable concession of legislative authority.

A second objection has been that the tax supplement forces a state or municipality for reasons of convenience to accept the flaws of the federal income tax. While admitting that the Internal Revenue Code has undergone more refinements than any state or local tax, opponents of the federal income tax may find fault with its rate structure, its deductions, or its exclusions.

VI—MUNICIPAL INCOME TAXATION AND THE NEW HAVEN AREA

The previous five sections of this chapter have examined the economic and legal problems and possibilities of the municipal income tax. In many ways, it is likely that the municipal income tax is superior to the local property tax, and in those areas where it may be deficient—notably administrative cost—a number of remedies are possible. This section assesses the arguments for and against the municipal income tax focusing on New Haven as the example and computes some short run effects of that tax using 1970 census data.

At present, the laws of Connecticut would prohibit New Haven from taxing income. The prohibition does not, however, derive from the state constitution: state enabling legislation is all that is required to permit Connecticut's towns to tax income. Ideally, such enabling legislation would include provisions to pool resources in the collection of the tax so as to lower the cost of administration, and it would also define income broadly so as to include rents, dividends, and capital gains in the tax base. Some legal questions may arise here, such as the preemption doctrine and permissible rate structures, and they should be thoroughly investigated prior to a final drafting of the legislation. A brief review of the arguments for and against the income tax, in light of New Haven's situation follows.

1. The municipal income tax is an elastic tax. New Haven, like many old eastern cities, has recently witnessed large increases in property tax mill rates. Under an income tax, the steady growth of national income would insure that rate increases would be much less dramatic, and because of that fact, perhaps more politically palatable.

2. The municipal income tax is probably less regressive than the property tax, at least in the short run. In the long run, high factor mobility may weaken any differences in the vertical equity of the two taxes. At any rate, given a broad definition of income and a graduated rate structure, the income tax can become progressive more easily than the property tax.

3. The income tax taxes equal income people equally as a matter of course. In this the property tax suffers: not only are there problems of assessment (New Haven reassesses only once in each decade), but there are also problems of tax-exempt property (30 percent of New Haven's gross grand list is tax-exempt). Being able to broaden the tax base to include tax-exempt properties and their employees is an important consideration.

4. The municipal income tax does not continue to be a burden for people whose command over resources declines. If one is elderly or unemployed, one's liability under an income tax declines. This phenomenon may cause financial problems in smaller, "company" towns since strikes or layoffs would cut sharply at the local government budget. However, New Haven has a fairly diverse industrial and business mix, and thus the city's coffers should not suffer unreasonably over the course of the business cycle, even if income tax rates remained constant.

5. The municipal income tax can be more expensive to administer than the property tax. This is true if a single city decides to administer an income tax on its own. However, if a number of municipalities comprising a metropolitan area join together to collect and administer income taxes, then the costs can be significantly reduced. A statewide operation can be even more efficient. Under these systems the costs of income tax collection are lower than those of property tax collection.

6.   The local property and income taxes are both economically inefficient. However, given the broader base of the income tax and its resulting lower rates, the inefficiency may be reduced under the income tax. This issue is a difficult one, however, and should be acknowledged as such.

7.   Differentials in income tax rates between towns, other things being equal, may provide stronger incentives for industry to relocate than do property tax rate differentials. Little is known of this fear of tax flight, and what is known is simply that taxes are secondary motives for industry location and that determining changes to the pattern of industry location is a very difficult task.

Even if an income tax were shown to be a significiant influence to location decisions, New Haven would probably suffer less than other cities. In Yale University, New Haven has a large, stationary employer. Other large New Haven employers (Southern New England Telephone, United Illuminating) are more or less tied to New Haven by virtue of large capital commitments. Still other employers (Armstrong Rubber, Sargent Hardware, Gant Shirt) enjoy new and modern plants which they will not abandon readily. Moreover, to the extent the tax base is broadened by including tax-exempt property and nonresident commuters, the tax bills paid by New Haven's industry will decline and thus weaken any potential urban flight based on tax differentials.

Tax Bill Estimates by Type of Property

In 1970, the net grand list for the city of New Haven was approximately $629 million. Of that total, 51.5 percent was attributable to industrial and commercial property taxation. The almost $324 million in business assessments were composed of buildings and personal property such as machines, furniture, tools, inventories, and special equipment such as cables and computers. The remaining $305 million of the net grand list could be viewed as assessments of residents, both owners and renters.

Only estimates can be made of the municipal income tax base, using 1970 census data. For our purposes, let us assume an income tax on all forms of income for residents, on earned income within the city for nonresidents, and on business earnings. Table 4-3 displays the relevant tax base data. Table 4-4 documents area commutation patterns.

In 1970, the city of New Haven raised approximately $40 million by the property tax. Business nominally paid over $20 million of that sum leaving slightly less to be divided among the city's home-owners, renters, and landlords. The city had 7,995 single-family, owner-occupied dwelling units in 1970 with a median value of $22,700. The stated assessment ratio is 60 percent so that median assessed value was $13,620. Also in 1970, there were 31,783 renter occupied units whose median contract rent was $1,284 per year.

With a property tax base of $629 million, the effective property tax rate needed to raise $40 million is about 0.0636. Thus, the median family in owner occupied housing could expect to pay $13,620 × 0.0636 = $866 in property tax in 1970. Assuming that taxes are at most 30 percent of rents, the median family in a rental unit could expect to bear $385 in property tax burden. It should be observed that the median family in a rental unit has a lower income than the median family in owner-occupied housing. With an income

Table 4-3. New Haven Income Tax Base Estimates—1970

Resident Income Tax Base	
New Haven resident families	33,275
New Haven mean family income	$10,444
New Haven resident income tax base	$347.5 million
Suburban Payroll Tax Base	
Area industrial payroll	$493.0 million
Area industrial employees	77,322
Wages per industrial worker	$ 6,377
Suburban residents working in New Haven	34,303
Suburban residents' New Haven payroll, assuming workers earn mean industrial wages	$218.8 million

Business Earnings Tax Base

This estimate is derived from national IRS figures on taxable business earnings for manufacturing, wholesaling, and retailing. Assumptions made: (a) Business is as profitable in New Haven as it is in the country as a whole, and (b) Profits per employee in all business (excluding government and nonprofit institutions) are the same as in manufacturing, wholesaling, and retailing.

Taxable business earnings estimate for New Haven	$158.2 million
Total Resident Income Tax Base	$505.7 million
Total Income Tax Base	$724.5 million

Source: 1970 Bureau of the Census, Area Statistics; 1967 Census of Manufacturing; 1967 Census of Business; 1969 Internal Revenue Service, Statistics of Income.

Table 4-4.   New Haven Area Commutation Patterns

Town	1971 Population	Workers Living In Town	Resident Workers Working in New Haven	Fraction Working In New Haven	Mean Family Income
Bethany	3,900	1,514	584	.39	$17,437
Branford	20,400	8,532	2,693	.32	14,074
East Haven	25,100	10,348	4,903	.47	11,605
Guilford	12,300	4,712	1,048	.22	14,757
Hamden	50,800	21,202	8,844	.42	14,191
New Haven	135,400	54,800	31,815	.58	10,444
No. Branford	11,000	4,186	1,376	.33	13,225
No. Haven	22,400	8,977	3,108	.35	15,142
Orange	13,900	5,337	1,565	.29	18,682
West Haven	53,600	22,743	8,238	.36	11,358
Woodbridge	7,900	3,030	1,340	.44	24,922
SMSA	356,700	145,381	65,514	.45	
Madison	10,500	3,209	604	.19	16,047
Labor Market	367,200	148,590	66,118	.44	

Summary Figures

Resident New Haven Workers
Working in New Haven   31,815
Working in Suburbs   22,985
                           54,800

Resident Suburban Workers
Working in New Haven   34,303
Working in Suburbs   59,507
                           93,810

tax base of $742.5 million, the effective income tax rate in 1970 would have been 0.0552. The median family with an income of $9,031 would have nominally paid only $499 in income tax. Business directly would have paid only about $8.75 million.

Tax Burdens Under Various Incidence Assumptions

As has been cautioned elsewhere in this chapter, a person's nominal tax liability (the tax bill paid) may not be equal to the actual tax burden he eventually bears. Using the tax base estimates of Table 4-3 without any qualifications might give a false picture of the real costs of adopting a municipal income tax. Tables 4-5 through 4-7 offer some short run tax burden estimates under a variety of assumptions and different tax schemes.

Table 4-5 assumes that the municipal income tax completely replaces the $40 million raised by the property tax in 1970. Table 4-6 employs the point of view that about one-quarter of the city government's expenditures can be viewed as expenditures on direct services to property and thus the property tax should be used as a rough user charge to finance those direct services. The remainder of the city's expenditures are assumed to be financed by the income tax.

Table 4-5. Short Run New Haven Tax Burdens—Municipal Income Tax Completely Replaces Property Tax

	Assumptions			
	1	*2*	*3*	*4*
Suburban competition	No	No	Yes	Yes
Workers bear payroll tax?	All	1/2	All	1/2
Firms bear profits tax?	Yes	Yes	Yes	Yes
Applicable Income Tax Base (Millions)	$724.5	$724.5	$505.7	$505.7
Applicable Tax Rates to Raise $40 Million				
On income	5.52%	5.52%	7.91%	7.91%
On property	0%	0%	0%	0%
Estimated Tax Burden on				
Median income family in city ($9031)	$499	$312[a]	$714	$446[a]
All business (Millions)	$ 8.73	$ 24.38	$ 12.51	$ 26.26

[a] Assumes Census-derived 1.78 workers per family, equal commuter and resident incomes, and that mean wage is also median wage.

Table 4-6. Short Run New Haven Tax Burdens—$10 Million (1/4 of $40 Million) Raised by Service-Related Property Tax and $30 Million Raised by Income Tax

	Assumptions			
	1	2	3	4
Suburban competition?	No	No	Yes	Yes
Workers bear payroll tax?	All	1/2	All	1/2
Firms bear profits tax?	Yes	Yes	Yes	Yes
Property tax bill equals burden?	Yes	Yes	Yes	Yes
Applicable Tax Bases (Millions)				
Property	$629	$629	$629	$629
Income	$724.5	$724.5	$505.7	$505.7
Applicable Tax Rates				
Property (to raise $10 million)	1.59%	1.59%	1.59%	1.59%
Income (to raise $30 million)	4.14%	4.14%	5.93%	5.93%
Estimated Tax Burden on				
Median income family in city ($9031)[a]	$673	$533	$835	$634
All business (Millions)[b]	$ 11.55	$ 16.75	$ 14.38	$ 24.69

[a] Assumes Census-derived 1.78 workers per family, equal commuter and resident incomes, that mean wage is also median wage, that median family spends 1/4 of income on housing services, that housing services constitute 12% of housing value, and that median family bears full burden of any property tax.

[b] Assumes business bears its full profits tax and property tax bills.

Table 4-7 adopts the position that the property and income taxes are properly viewed as taxes on factors and thus (for reasons of economic efficiency) should be levied at the same rate. To make this estimate, both taxes are put on a flow basis—that is, the income tax is viewed as a tax on a person's yearly command over resources, and the property tax is viewed not as a tax on the value of a house but as a tax on the yearly flow of housing services attributable to the house. Annual property services are assumed to be 12 percent of full market value.

For each table's computations various simple incidence assumptions are made. One choice of asssumptions turns on whether suburbs tax income at the same rate as New Haven, thereby foreclosing the suburban tax base to New Haven's use. Another choice of assumption is concerned with whether workers bear the payroll tax or whether firms do.

Table 4-7. Short Run New Haven Tax Burdens—Property and Income Taxes Levied at Same Rate on Income and Property Services Flows

| | Assumptions | | | |
	1	2	3	4
Suburban competition?	No	No	Yes	Yes
Workers bear payroll tax?	All	1/2	All	1/2
Firms bear profits tax?	Yes	Yes	Yes	Yes
Property tax bill equals burden?	Yes	Yes	Yes	Yes
Applicable Tax Bases (Millions)				
Property	$126.1	$ 75.5	$ 75.5	$ 75.5
Income	$724.5	$724.5	$505.7	$505.7
Applicable Tax Rates				
Property	4.70%	5.00%	6.33%	6.88%
Income	5.00%	5.00%	6.88%	6.88%
Estimated Tax Burden on				
Median income family in city ($9031)[a]	$531	$318	$715	$429
All business (Millions)[b]	$ 10.40	$ 23.72	$ 12.97	$ 26.49

[a]Assumes Census-derived 1.78 workers per family, equal commuter and resident incomes, that mean wage is also median wage, that median family spends 1/4 of income on housing services, that housing services constitute 12% of housing value, and that median family bears full burden of any property tax.

[b]Assumes business bears its full profits tax and property tax bills.

The reasons for differences in tax burdens between the various tax schemes and the simple property tax should be clear. Under a property tax, businesses and homeowners probably pay dearly. However, by being a renter and consuming less housing, one can avoid much of the burden of the property tax. Under an income tax, homeowners probably make out much better. So long as businesses do not have to pay too much in additional wages (which is unlikely), under reasonable incidence assumptions they also make out better under a municipal income tax. The burden of the income tax, as compared to the burden of the property tax, shifts to suburbanites, to higher income city residents, and to renters. Where incentives existed under the property tax to avoid the tax by renting and consuming less housing, those incentives have been removed under a municipal income tax.

Of course, if the suburbs surrounding New Haven retaliate with income taxes of their own, less of the burden of New Haven's tax will be borne by suburbanites. Less of the tax will also be borne by business since the extra wages business must pay depend upon tax rate differentials between towns. New Haven residents will thus bear more of the burden of their income tax than they did prior to the suburban taxes. Nevertheless, the municipal income tax will in many ways remain a fairer tax than the property tax, and if suburban income tax rates are not as high as the New Haven rate, New Haven can expect to gain at least some suburban revenues from commuters. Moreover, the tax base will be broader in any case because of the inclusion of previously tax-exempt property, and that is a considerable advantage in itself.

In sum, the municipal income tax does indeed appear to be an attractive alternative to New Haven's present sole reliance on the property tax. Net income will almost surely be redistributed among various groups within the metropolitan area as a result of the income tax's imposition, and this may argue for its gradual rather than abrupt phase-in. Even so, there are many sound features to municipal income taxation which recommend it for much more widespread and serious attention than it has received in many states.

Efficiency in Service Provision

Chapter 5

Refuse Collection Policy

Peter Kemper
John M. Quigley

The problems of public service provision are conceptually similar for a wide range of particular public services. If a service is provided publicly at the local level, it is usually due to externalities in consumption, economies of scale in production, or because ethical norms are violated by private provision. In these instances, local policy makers must select the type and level of output and decide on a pricing or financing mechanism. In addition, if the local government produces and distributes the service itself, it faces all the operational decisions of other business organizations.

To address any of these policy questions for a particular local service, it is critical to define and measure output, to consider the "publicness" of this output, to relate alternative levels of output to their input resources, and to investigate the nature of consumer demand for the "product." Because local services are so heterogeneous, because output is so difficult to measure, because spillovers and externalities are so important—and finally because hard data are difficult to obtain, it is not surprising that there have been few systematic analyses of these issues, even for a single service.

Chapters Five through Seven share a common focus in addressing the conceptual and measurement issues for three particular public services for a single city. None of the services investigated—refuse collection, fire protection, and police services, which together account for 15 to 20 percent of local budgets—is consciously provided by the public sector on distributional grounds, yet each of them indicates, in slightly different ways, the class of conceptually similar issues in the provision of local services.

The analysis of these specific local services begins by considering residential refuse collection. There are good reasons for investigating this service first. The output provided by the service is reasonably easy to define and measure; the output is a relatively private good, making it a logical candidate for user charge financing.

The first part of this chapter considers the case for user charge financing of collection services in some detail and, based on data from New Haven, provides quantitative evidence on the importance of several key issues. The second part of the chapter presents estimates of the cost function for municipal refuse collection and explores several policy applications.

FINANCING BY USER CHARGES

Before user charges can be intelligently discussed, the services for which charges are to be considered must be carefully defined. Defining the output of refuse collection activity is easier than for most services provided by municipalities, but it is not without some complications. The obvious definition is the collection of a given amount of refuse at a particular location and its transportation to a disposal site. Additional dimensions of service are the frequency of collection and the location of pickup (back-of-house or curbside).

Beyond these obvious output measures lie two other explicit objectives, which are extremely difficult to measure: the elimination of health hazards and the reduction of street and yard litter. Presumably the achievement of these latter objectives is highly (though not perfectly) correlated with the collection of a specified amount of refuse from a particular location. Thus, we measure service output by the quantity of refuse collected with a specified frequency of collection and location of pickup, but in several points in the subsequent discussion we must explicitly address the question of externalities (such as adverse neighborhood effects if refuse is not regularly collected).

Efficiency

Although user charges are not commonly imposed for municipal refuse collection, economic principles suggest that user charges would improve resource allocation in the public sector. By giving consumers the choice of the service they consume, and charging them for it, consumers are given an incentive to economize on the resources of collection agencies, improving the mix of collection services that is provided. In contrast, if the government chooses the type of service provided, it has no practical way of evaluating alternative mixes of service, and even if it did, the government would have very little incentive to do so.

Allocative efficiency is achieved when two principles are observed. First, each resident must be charged the marginal cost incurred in providing the service he consumes. Second, when marginal cost is below average cost, the total benefits of providing the service to all residents must exceed the total costs; otherwise, the service should not be provided at all. Application of these principles is complicated by the existence of three dimensions of service and by consideration of public health and littering objectives. The efficiency principles require that residents be free to alter their consumption along each of these dimensions, and that they be charged accordingly. For each dimension of service, the efficiency principles have slightly different implications.

For differences in the location of pickup, the first principle requires that residents who select back-of-house collection be charged the additional cost of picking up and returning containers to the back of the house. These charges would provide an incentive for households to substitute their own labor for that of the collection agency. Since the marginal cost and average cost of this service are undoubtedly approximately equal, the second principle imposes no additional constraints. For differences in the amount of refuse collected, the first principle implies that households should be charged the marginal cost of collecting the refuse they generate. This charge provides incentives to reduce refuse generation and to recycle the refuse generated. At the same time, however, it provides an incentive for increased littering and accumulation of refuse.

Whether such a charge would increase economic efficiency depends upon the trade-off between the benefit of reduced generation and the cost of additional littering and health hazards. In high density neighborhoods, these externalities may be quite important, thus rendering a user charge inefficient unless minimum standards are also enforced. In low density neighborhoods, however, the imposition of tonnage or volume-related user charges may improve allocative efficiency. Because of the serious health hazards if refuse is not collected, it is reasonable to assume that the second efficiency principle (the benefit-cost criterion) is satisfied.

Applying the efficiency principles to the frequency of collection is more complicated. Once a jurisdiction has decided to offer twice-a-week service, then residents should be charged only the marginal cost of collecting their own refuse. But the city must decide whether to provide twice-a-week service according to the overall benefit-cost criterion. If the demand curve for frequency of collection were known, it would be possible to compute the total benefits and costs of twice-a-week as compared to once-a-week service, and to provide twice-a-week service if total benefits exceeded total costs. However, once the decision to cover the routes twice a week has been made, it is inefficient to charge residents for the more frequent service; they should be charged only the incremental cost of stopping at their houses, but this cost would already be reflected in a tonnage charge.

Thus it is the second efficiency principle that motivates the design of the system of charges. An imperfect way of designing such a system is to allow residents a choice of twice-a-week service, charging them the average cost of the more frequent service. Specifically, this charge would equal the difference between the cost of providing twice-a-week and that of once-a-week service, divided by the number of residents who choose twice-a-week service on any collection route. This system of charges would ensure that the total benefits exceed total costs if twice-a-week service is provided at all (since consumers reveal that they are willing to pay for the more frequent service). However, in some cases where total benefits of twice-a-week service exceed total costs, it would not be provided. Nonetheless, the system would provide a gross improvement in efficiency by ensuring that cities would not provide more frequent collection unless it were desired.

In order to reach a conclusion about which charges are practical, we must consider any additional administrative costs imposed by user charge financing. The administrative costs of charging for differences in pickup location and frequency cannot be prohibitive because private collectors do so without obvious difficulty. Charges for the amount of refuse generated would probably be more costly to administer, but again some private firms and municipalities do base charges on the number of containers collected. In short, a recognition of implementation costs reinforces our conclusion, based on efficiency considerations, that user charges that vary by frequency and service level would improve economic efficiency, but that user charges based upon volume or tonnage may not be efficient.

Equity
Efficiency is not the only relevant consideration in financing decisions. Another is the equity of the charges. The cost of refuse collection is small relative to total income; the effect of user charge financing on the distribution of income is hardly the most significant equity issue of general governmental policy. Nonetheless, it may be a serious issue in refuse collection policy, because residents may ex-

pect to receive the service "free" of charge and because there is a presumption that general revenue financing, when compared with user charge financing, benefits the poor.

A review of the public administration literature indicates that the incidence of user charges is indeed an important consideration in the choice of financing method. For example, in discussing the advantages of general revenue financing, the American Public Works Association (APWA) says that under such a system "the cost of a collection operation is distributed more nearly on an ability to pay basis" than under alternative methods.[1] In discussing the "service charge" alternative, the APWA cites the following as the major disadvantage of such charges:

> Refuse service charges levied according to the benefits received are regressive. The amount of refuse does not vary with the ability to pay taxes; poor families may have more refuse per capita than wealthy ones.[2]

This view, however, confuses two issues. First, it fails to compare the incidence of charges with the incidence of the alternative source of local revenues, typically the property tax. And second, it assumes that there is no systematic relationship between refuse generation (hence the demand for collection) and the incomes of residents (hence their consumption levels).

How regressive are user charges for refuse collection? We can provide no evidence on the incidence of charges that vary with type of service or frequency, but in both dimensions the income elasticity of demand for service is presumably greater than the income elasticity of the amount of refuse generated. Our evidence on the incidence of charges varying with the amount of refuse generated suggests that the imposition of these charges would be progressive when compared to general revenue financing.

Our evidence is based on data for the city of New Haven, which maintains records on the amount of refuse collected along each of its 33 routes. By matching information on incomes and family composition from the U.S. Census, we estimated the relationship between household refuse generation in 1972, household income, and family size. The results (reported in Table 5-1) suggest an income elasticity of refuse generation of about .76.

The bottom part of the table presents the estimate of the income elasticity of refuse generation (and hence charges that vary by tonnage) as a proportion of income. Also included are estimates of the income elasticity of property taxes as a proportion of income derived from existing empirical studies of the incidence of property taxation.

Table 5-1.   Refuse Generation and Incidence of User Charges for Refuse Collection

---

A. Estimates of Refuse Generation from Route Data in New Haven, Conn.

$$Q = -8.84 + 0.76Y + 1.90P$$
$$\quad\ (5.88)\ \ (4.64)\quad (6.92)$$

$$R^2 = .72$$
$$df = 30 \text{ routes}$$

where
Q = per household refuse generation (in tons)
Y = median household income
P = average persons per household
and all variables are in logarithmic form.

B. Estimated Progressivity of Financing Refuse Collection through Property Taxes and through User Charges on the Amount of Refuse Collected

	Estimated Income Elasticity of Charges as a Proportion of Income
User Charges	-0.24
Property Tax	
Homeowners	
Netzer	-2.63
Morgan	-1.82
Renters	
Netzer	-1.42
Morgan	-1.68
Combined Owners and Renters	
Pechman/Okner	-3.05/-4.00

Source: Computed from Dick Netzer, *Economics of the Property Tax,* The Brookings Institution, 1966, tables 3-6 and 3-8; James N. Morgan, et al, *Income and Welfare in the United States,* New York: McGraw-Hill, 1962, tables 19-1 and 19-6; Joseph A. Pechman and Benjamin A. Okner, *Who Bears the Tax Burden?,* The Brookings Institution, 1974, table 4-8, Variant 3-b/lc. All estimates were obtained by regression analysis of data over the income range $0-$20,000. Table presents the coefficient b estimated from the regression log $T/Y = a + b \log Y$, where T is average property tax payment and Y is annual income.

As compared with a proportional income tax, where the elasticity is 0, a tonnage charge would be slightly regressive. However, property taxes appear far more regressive. Thus, on balance, replacing the property tax with a charge on the amount of refuse collected would be highly progressive. In short, user charges for any dimension of service appear unlikely to be regressive relative to property tax financing.

Revenue from Tax Exempt Institutions

Another motivation for imposing user charges is to raise revenue from tax exempt institutions. One jurisdiction in Connecticut, Middletown, has imposed service charges with precisely this motivation by organizing a special district for the sole purpose of refuse collection. This special district makes charges to properties of various classes (e.g., "churches," "schools"). City officials report that 3.9 per cent of the total revenue collected through these charges comes from tax-exempt property, indicating that a modest amount of additional revenue can be expected by extending the "tax" base in this way. Although economists are not inclined to attach much weight to arguments based solely on revenue considerations, city officials facing budget deficits clearly do.

Federal Income Tax Deductibility

The choice of financing method may affect the federal income tax deductibility of payments for refuse collection. If refuse collection is financed by a tax (any uniform ad valorem levy, except special assessment levies), the amount is deductible from gross income for federal income tax computation. If, however, collection is financed by a charge that varies with any other characteristics of the property (such as structure type), or with the location of pickup, frequency of collection, or amount of refuse collected, such a charge does not qualify as a deductible personal expense. As a result, a dollar of municipal expenditure on refuse collection financed by taxes costs the homeowner who itemizes deductions less than a dollar. This does not change the real resource cost of refuse collection, but, by transferring some of the tax burden to the federal level, it makes property tax financing more attractive from the city resident's perspective than user charges.

How important is this federal tax incentive for financing out of general revenues? The magnitude of the saving available to any individual depends upon his marginal tax bracket and on whether he itemizes his deductions. Table 5-2, which presents the marginal tax brackets associated with income classes, indicates that a community composed entirely of households in the $20,000-$25,000 income bracket who itemize deductions would have a tax savings of 28 cents per dollar of property tax paid.

More generally, the percentage of federal tax savings resulting from general revenue financing for a jurisdiction depends upon the income distribution and the proportion of residents who itemize deductions. Table 5-2 indicates the income distribution of New

Table 5-2.   Estimated Tax Saving Due to Federal Deductibility of Local Taxes

Income Class (thousands of dollars)	Marginal Tax Rate[a]	New Haven			Woodbridge		
		Number of Households[b]	Estimated Proportion Itemizing[c]	Tax Savings	Number of Households[b]	Estimated Proportion Itemizing[c]	Tax Savings
<4	.14	21,933	.12	.02	71	.49	.07
4–5.9	.16	6,998	.19	.03	58	.60	.10
6–9.9	.19	12,295	.26	.05	149	.72	.14
10–14.9	.22	9,690	.40	.09	345	.83	.18
15–19.9	.25	4,931	.55	.14	617	.89	.22
20–24.9	.28		.55	.16		.89	.25
25–29.9	.32	1,338	.66	.21	548	.95	.30
30–49.9	.39		.66	.26		.95	.37
50–99.9	.53	283	.66	.35	161	.95	.50
100–199.9	.62		.66	.41		.95	.59
200+	.70		.66	.46		.95	.66
Average federal tax savings to households per dollar of residential property tax				.06			.27
Owner occupied property as a proportion of all taxable property[d]				.15			.80
Average federal tax savings to homeowners per dollar of total property tax				.01			.21

[a] U.S. Department of the Treasury, Internal Revenue Service, *Statistics of Income 1971, Individual Income Tax Returns*, Publication 79, Washington, D.C.: U.S. Government Printing Office, 1973, p. 350.

[b] U.S. Bureau of the Census, *1970 Census of Housing* "General Housing Characteristics" Final Report HC(1) A8, Connecticut, Washington, D.C.: U.S. Government Printing Office, 1971, Tables 10 & 24.

[c] For New Haven, the estimated proportion of households itemizing deductions is the proportion of homeowners, by income class found in U.S. Bureau of the Census. *1970 Metropolitan Housing Characteristics*, Washington, D.C.: U.S. Government Printing Office, 1972, Tables A–3, B–3, C–3. (For Woodbridge, the proportion used is that for metropolitan area residents living outside New Haven and West Haven.)

[d] State of Connecticut, *Information Relative to the Assessment and Collection of Taxes*, Public Document No. 48, Hartford, State of Connecticut, 1970.

Haven (with a median household income of $5,943, including families and unrelated individuals) and that of the high income suburb of Woodbridge (median income $17,956). Also presented are estimates of the proportion of homeowners by income class, a proxy for the fraction itemizing deductions. As the table indicates, not only are household incomes and marginal tax brackets higher in Woodbridge, but home ownership rates—and hence the proportion likely to itemize deductions—are also higher.

If we consider a service provided only to residential properties financed by a tax on those properties alone, the weighted average of the tax savings from financing through general revenues is .27 in Woodbridge, indicating that local residents would pay only 73 percent of the costs of a service provided to all residences. The corresponding figure for New Haven indicates that residents would pay 94 percent of the costs of this service. On the other hand, if we consider the same service to residential properties financed by a general tax on *all* properties—residential, commercial, and industrial— the average tax saving to residents also depends upon the proportion of taxable property devoted to commercial, industrial, and rental property, since either taxes or user charges are deductible as ordinary business expenses for these types of properties.

In New Haven, if a given service provided to residences were financed out of general revenues instead of by user charges, the dollar cost to local residents and businesses would be reduced by about 1 percent. In the nearby suburb, the corresponding tax saving would be more than 20 percent. In short, although it is not clear whether people fully perceive it, a substantial tax incentive exists to finance refuse collection—or any public service—through property taxes or other ad valorem taxes. For richer communities, the incentive appears to be quite strong.

Conclusion

We conclude that there is a strong case for the imposition of user charges for refuse collection. In particular, it appears that user charges that vary with the location of pickup and the frequency of collection are likely to result in an improved allocation of resources. Charges that vary with the amount of refuse generated by households could also lead to improved efficiency, but because they create an incentive for increased littering, they should not be imposed in high density areas.

One strong argument against user charges, however, is that, unlike property taxes, they do not qualify as personal deductions for federal income tax purposes. Consequently, from the perspective of city residents, user charges are more costly than property taxes, especially for high income residents. Given the potential efficiency gains, this provision of the Internal Revenue Code merits review for elimination of the artificial incentive.

COLLECTION COSTS

As noted in the introduction, little is known about the parameters of the cost functions for the services provided by local governments. In large part, this uncertainty arises because the attributes of public services, or the output units, are so difficult to measure. We have noted that these measurement problems are less severe for refuse collection services, and in this section we present quantitative evidence on the cost function for refuse collection services using data from the city of New Haven. After presenting the empirical estimates, we perform some simple policy analyses based upon the results.

Estimation of the Cost Function

Residential solid waste collection as presently performed is a rather simple production process, approximately described as a production process using fixed input proportions. The inputs typically consist of a compactor truck, a driver, and two laborers. The truck stops at a residence, the laborers get the containers and empty them into the compactor, and the truck moves on to the next house. When the truck is filled, the load is driven to the disposal site and dumped, and the truck returns to resume pickups. Thus the total time spent producing the service consists of two distinct parts, which may be described as the "pickup time" along the route (the time spent emptying cans and driving between units) and the "haul time" (the time spent hauling the load to the disposal site, dumping it, and returning to the collection route).

By describing production as a process using fixed factor proportions we do not mean to suggest either that there are no possibilities for factor substitution or that the presently used factor proportions are necessarily most efficient. But we do assert that for empirical analysis of existing operations, the assumption of fixed factor proportions approximates observed behavior, at least within the city of New Haven. This assumption may not apply, however, for some cities with wide variations in residential densities; the greater driving distance between pickups make two-man crews more costly than one-man crews in very low density areas.

Although the production process is the same, collection cost will nevertheless vary across routes in the city. Variations in residential density (which determine the distance between pickup units) may affect the time spent collecting each ton along the route. Variations in hauling distance may affect the time spent hauling. Moreover, inefficient route layouts and other managerial inefficiencies may lead to variations in output per unit input that would not otherwise exist. For all these reasons, output per unit of input will, in general, not be constant across locations, even though the actual production process is the same.

A simple model based on this description begins by recognizing that average cost per ton can be written as the product of cost per unit time and collection time per ton, and that cost per unit time can be divided into labor and capital cost:

$$AC = \frac{TC}{T} \cdot \frac{T}{Q} = (c_L + c_K)\frac{T}{Q} \tag{1}$$

where

AC = average cost per ton

TC = total cost

T = total time spent collecting

Q = total tonnage collected

c_L = cost of labor per hour, including wages, fringe benefits, and direct supervisory costs

c_K = rental of trucks per hour actually used, including interest, depreciation, operation, and maintenance

The identity given by equation (1) states that the cost per ton is simply the hourly cost of labor and capital multiplied by the hours required to collect each ton. For a given city using the same production process everywhere, c_L and c_K can be assumed constant. The time per ton can be divided further into the pickup time per ton and the haul time per ton:

$$\frac{T}{Q} = \frac{T_p}{Q} + \frac{T_h}{N} \cdot \frac{N}{Q} \tag{2}$$

where

T_p = total pickup time

T_h = total haul time

N = total number of trips to the disposal site

Combining (1) and (2) gives:

$$AC = (c_L + c_K) \left(\frac{T}{Q} \right) = (c_L + c_K) \left(\frac{T_p}{Q} + \frac{T_h}{N} \cdot \frac{N}{Q} \right) \qquad (3)$$

As it stands, equation (3) is simply an identity; it becomes a useful behavioral equation when the variables that affect pickup time per ton (T_p/Q) and haul time per run (T_h/N) are specified. The major factors that affect pickup time per ton include the density along any route, the weather, the type of service provided, and the type of containers used. Only the first two factors vary within New Haven. Haul time per run is a function of the haul mileage, the type of roads traversed, the procedures at the disposal site, and possibly the type of vehicles used. Again, only the first two vary within New Haven. Thus:

$$\frac{T}{Q} = \frac{T_p}{Q} + \frac{T_h}{N} \cdot \frac{N}{Q} = f(D,S) + g(H) \cdot \frac{N}{Q} \qquad (4)$$

where

D = density of collection

S = snow

H = haul miles

T/Q = time required to collect a unit of refuse

N/Q = number of hauls to incinerator per ton of refuse

Conceivably, equation (4) could be estimated from a time and motion study. Observers could accompany each crew, counting the number of cans, clocking the time spent at each task, measuring mileages, etc. From data collected in this manner, some specification of equation (4) could be approximated. There are several serious problems with this approach, however. In the first place, such a study would be extraordinarily expensive even to obtain estimates for a single city. Second, workers are notoriously resistant to such observations; unionized workers in the public sector are unlikely to be less resistant. Third, the effect of being observed may change behavior, making direct estimates unreliable. An alternative to a time and motion study is statistical estimation by regression analysis.

Much of the information required for statistical estimation of equation (4) was available from city records that are generated as a matter of routine in New Haven.[a] These data were used to estimate alternative linear specifications of equation (4) by generalized least squares,[b] using the route covered by each truck on each day as the unit of observation. Equation (5) presents the regression results using the reciprocal specification of density,[c] and disaggregating haul miles into mileage along city streets (M_S) and mileage along interstate highways (M_I). T-ratios appear in parentheses.

[a]We are grateful to several officials of the city of New Haven, especially Mr. Sidney Zolot and Mr. C.W. Gamble, for providing us with access to data maintained by the city and for acquainting us with the operation of refuse collection activities in New Haven. The Public Works Department records the truck identification number, the time of day, and the weight of each load dumped at its incinerator. Thus for each route serviced on each day, it was possible to obtain information on the total tonnage collected, the number of loads, and the time of day that the last load was dumped. For each route, the haul mileage and the route mileage were obtained from maps supplied by the Public Works Department. The number of inches of snowfall was obtained from the Weather Bureau. In this way, the refuse collection experience for New Haven for 1972 was assembled. The sample consisted of 2,791 observations on the collection activity for each route day for the fiscal year.

Unfortunately, the dependent variable cannot be measured with precision. The time that the last load is dumped is not the time that the crew is actually finished because each crew must park and service its truck. This omitted time is probably a small constant, which is independent of the tonnage collected. More important, the actual starting time for each crew is not recorded; consequently, a starting time must be assumed to interpret the intercept of a linear regression estimate of (4). The estimate intercept will include any error in the assumed starting time.

For example, if we assume that the starting time is 5:00 a.m. when the true starting time is 6:00 a.m., then the intercept will be overestimated by one hour. Neither of these problems is serious, however, unless the omitted times are both variable and correlated with the explanatory variables. The starting time is undoubtedly variable, and the time required to park and wash the vehicle may exhibit variation as well. But there is no reason to expect these omitted times to be correlated with the explanatory variables. Thus the principal effect of the errors in the dependent variable will be to increase the variance of the error term and reduce the goodness of fit of the estimated regression, and not to bias the coefficient.[3]

[b]Plots of the residuals from the ordinary least squares estimates of equation (4) strongly suggest that the residual variance increases with the elapsed time to the last weigh-in. This is not implausible, since long total collection times may be associated with unusually long break times, vehicle malfunctions, breakdowns, and both early and late starting times. The regressions reported above were corrected for heteroskedasticity by applying generalized least squares using the reciprocal of elapsed time as weights for the observations. As noted the actual starting time for collection crews is not recorded; it was estimated by subtracting the average elapsed time between the first and second loads (137 minutes) from the average time the first load is dumped (6:52 a.m.). The estimated starting time is thus 4:35 a.m. or 275 minutes after midnight.

[c]This specification is one of several estimated, all with similar results.

$$\frac{T}{Q} = \underset{(16.82)}{6.158} + \underset{(33.22)}{14.370}\,\frac{1}{D} + \underset{(0.20)}{0.027S} + \underset{(12.85)}{35.310}\,\frac{N}{Q} \tag{5}$$

$$+ \underset{(9.82)}{5.924}\,\frac{N}{Q}\,M_S + \underset{(4.84)}{2.132}\,\frac{N}{Q}\,M_I$$

$R^2 = .54$

df = 2,785 route days

The simple model of refuse collection explains 54 percent of the variance in average collection times, and, with the exception of the variable representing snow on the ground during collection, all the coefficients are highly significant. Since New Haven provides only curbside collection, it is not surprising that the presence of snow has little or no effect on average collection times. Haul mileage significantly affects the total time required to collect a ton of refuse. The results indicate that an additional mile of hauling on city streets increases average time by about six minutes per ton, while an additional mile of hauling along interstate highways increases average time by about two minutes.

These results provide strong evidence that there are economies of density in residential refuse collection. The elasticity of cost with respect to density (calculated at the means) is .3; that is, a 1 percent increase in collection density reduces average collection time by about three-tenths of a percent. The magnitude of these economies of density decline as collection density is further increased. At twice the density observed in New Haven, the elasticity is about .2, while at half the density, the estimated elasticity is .6. These results are illustrated in Figure 5-1, which presents a plot of the predicted collection time, having controlled for all variables except density, versus collection density and the estimated regression equation.

To use these empirical results to obtain the cost function for residential refuse collection in New Haven, estimates of capital and labor costs per unit time are required. Study of New Haven's expenditures provides estimates of the economic costs of labor, capital, and overhead for New Haven. These cost estimates are summarized in Table 5-3. Total annual cost of residential refuse collection is estimated to be about $641,000 or roughly $.83 per minute of collection time. When the small overhead expenditure is allocated in proportion to direct labor and capital expenses, the cost of labor is an estimated $.64 per minute and that of capital, $.19 per minute. The labor costs

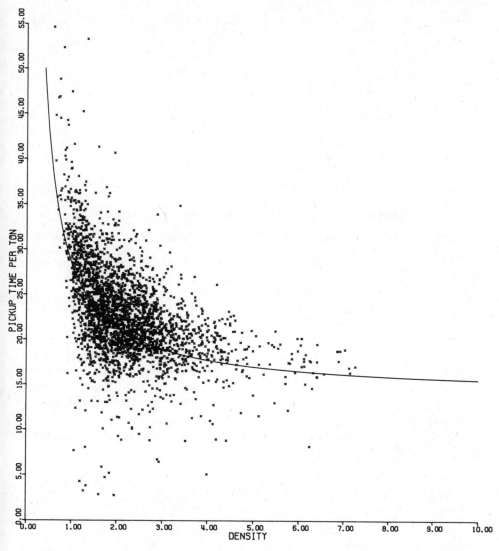

Figure 5-1. Average Collection Time Versus Density for New Haven Sample

are much higher than the hourly wage rates paid laborers because they include indirect labor costs such as fringe benefits and supervisor wages, and because they are based on the time actually spent collecting, not including the paid time before collection begins or after the last load is dumped.

Using these estimates, the parameters of the cost function for New Haven based on the regression results may be expressed as:

$$AC = (c_L + c_K) \left(\frac{T}{Q} \right) = 5.11 + 11.92 \frac{1}{D} + 0.02S \qquad (6)$$

$$+ 29.31 \frac{N}{Q} + 4.91 \frac{N}{Q} M_S + 1.77 \frac{N}{Q} M_I$$

where, as before

AC = average cost per ton of refuse

D = density of residential collection (tons per mile)

S = snow on ground at 7:00 a.m.

M_S = haul miles on city streets from route to incinerator

M_I = haul miles on interstate highway from route to incinerator

N/Q = number of trips to incinerator per ton of refuse.

Some Implications of the Cost Estimates

This cost function can be used to provide crude answers to some simple questions of public concern.

Moving the Disposal Site. In Connecticut, as in many other states, environmental protection authorities at the state level are becoming increasingly concerned with disposal facilities. Several coordinated disposal plans have been recommended to accommodate future refuse generation. Typically, these plans involve major reorganization and consolidation of facilities, moving the disposal site

Table 5-3. Estimates of Refuse Collection Costs per Minute for New Haven in 1972

	Category	*Total Cost*	*Cost per minute*
A. Overhead cost not	Overhead	$ 19,016	$0.02
allocated to labor and	Direct labor	476,600	0.62
capital	Direct capital	145,775	0.19
Total		$641,391	$0.83
B. Overhead costs allocated	Labor	$491,166	$0.64
proportionally to labor	Capital	150,225	0.19
and capital			
Total		$641,391	$0.83

Source: Peter Kemper and John M. Quigley, *The Economics of Refuse Collection*, Cambridge, Mass.: Ballinger, 1976.

further from the city center and increasing the hauling distance for every load dumped at the incinerator. This clearly will increase collection cost. Assuming that labor, capital, and overhead costs per unit time do not change,[d] and that the number of tons per load does not change, the change in total cost for each mile that the disposal site is moved can be calculated from equation (6) to be approximately $30,000.[e] This simple example indicates that there is a nontrivial interdependence between disposal practices and collection costs. According to these estimates, total collection costs increase up to 4.7 percent for each mile the disposal site is moved out of the city. Because of the assumption of constant cost per unit time, this estimate is an upper bound, especially for large increases in hauling distance where it would reduce cost to change the input mix or production technology.

Reducing the Frequency of Collection. In New Haven refuse is presently collected twice weekly from each eligible dwelling unit. Is it reasonable to reduce the frequency of collection to cut cost? While we are unable to estimate the change in benefits resulting from reduction in pickup frequency (due to possible public health hazards, pollution, and so forth), the cost function permits an estimate of the cost savings, at least in a rather crude fashion.

Reducing collection frequency reduces collection cost per ton for three reasons. First, since more refuse is collected on each pass over a given route, the effective tonnage density on each route is increased, reducing collection time per ton. Second, the reduction of pickup frequency may reduce the total amount of refuse generated, for reasons which are not well understood.[4] Third (at least in this city), reducing the frequency of refuse collection would simplify the prob-

---

[d]This is a strong assumption, especially in the short run. Labor costs per hour probably will not change with an increase in haul mileage. Although it is possible that effective hourly wages might go down slightly (since hauling requires less effort than collecting along the route), it seems more reasonable to assume that contracts will be renegotiated to reflect the increased labor time at the same effective wage. In the very short run, increased hauling would have no impact on total labor cost because the contract binds the union to a fixed total payment under the incentive system. In this case the only change in costs would be capital cost. Overhead costs per unit time will probably not change very much as a result of a change in haul mileage. Capital costs per unit time may change, according to the following argument. Total capital costs will increase by the mileage-related operating expenses only. This would imply a drop in the capital cost per unit time. On the other hand, in the long run, routes may be redesigned and new trucks purchased, returning to the original number of trucks per work day and thus to the same capital cost per unit time.

[e]This is calculated as follows: $\Delta TC = Q \, \Delta AC = Q \, \alpha_6 \dfrac{N}{Q} \Delta M_I = \alpha_6 \, N \, \Delta M_I$.

The number of runs per year is approximately 8,520 and a two-mile change in round trip interstate haul mileage implies: $\Delta TC = 1.77 \times 8520 \times 2 = \$30,200$.

lem of route design. Presently the routes covered on Mondays and Thursdays are identical, even though the amount of refuse varies substantially on different days. (There are three days between Monday and Thursday and four between Thursday and Monday.) Consequently, if Monday routes are designed efficiently, Thursday routes are almost surely designed inefficiently. The obvious solution is to have different route layouts on the two days, but this proves administratively difficult.

The cost reduction due to the first type of saving—i.e., that due to increased density, is approximately $160,000, a 25 percent reduction in total cost.[f] Several qualifications that make service reduction more attractive should be noted. First, as noted above, the savings estimate is biased downward because two additional sources of cost reduction are ignored. Second, if the reduction in frequency did in fact reduce refuse generation (and not merely increase littering), the demand on the overburdened incinerator would be reduced. Third, reducing collection frequency would reduce the household labor required to place cans at the curb and to clean up after collection. In short, while the cost savings must be weighed against an unmeasured reduction in benefits, switching to once-a-week collection appears to reduce costs substantially.

THE NEED FOR GOVERNMENT INTERVENTION

The shape of the estimated cost function has broader implications for the organization of the refuse collection sector. The evidence of substantial economies of density implies that collection of refuse should not be left to unregulated markets. Because of these economies it is inefficient to have several firms competing along the same route, since the repeated coverage of the same route reduces effective density. Moreover, private firms have an incentive to eliminate this inefficiency by dividing up the city so there is no overlap among the routes covered. But, having divided up the city into "territories," they are likely to succumb to the temptation to charge monopoly prices.

[f]This is calculated as follows:

$$\Delta TC = Q \, \Delta AC = Q \, \alpha_2 \, \Delta \frac{1}{D} = Q\alpha_2 \, \frac{\Delta M_R}{Q} = \alpha_2 \Delta M_R = \alpha_2 \, \frac{1}{2} M_R$$

where M_R represents route mileage. Since annual route mileage is approximately 26,900 miles, $\Delta TC = 11.92 \times 0.5 \times 26,900 = \$160,000$.

In short, the existence of economies of density implies that government intervention is required to take advantage of these economies of density on the one hand and to eliminate the potential for monopoly on the other. This intervention could take the form of government provision, regulation of a franchised monopoly, or contracting with private firms.

✳ *Chapter 6*

Fire Fighting Benefits

Malcolm Getz
Robert A. Leone

In 1972 municipal governments in the United States spent almost $2.6 billion for fire fighting services. For the typical city government these expenditures represented close to 15 percent of all locally collected tax revenues. Fire protection is about 4 percent of locally collected revenues for all local governments considered together.

Unlike many public services, there is little disagreement about the primary objectives of the fire service: "Fire Fighters Fight Fires and Save Lives."[a] There is even a general acceptance of the principal methods available to achieve these ends. Although it is quite difficult to measure losses prevented and lives saved, these benefits are almost certainly more tractable than are the often more intangible benefits from other mainstays of local municipal budgets, for instance, police protection or public education. Further, data are obtainable on fire losses by various types of property and on fire service expenditures both over time and across a sample of municipal governments. In sum, the importance of fire service expenditures in local budgets, the relative tractability of benefits, and the availability of relevant data all combine to make the fire service an excellent candidate for benefit analysis.

This chapter reports the results of two empirical attempts to measure the benefits of fire services in New Haven. The first exercise examines data describing individual fires within the city and attempts to assign benefits to classes of properties by correlating fire

[a]Slogan of the International Association of Fire Fighters.

related losses to structure and neighborhood characteristics. The second exercise uses aggregate information about fire loss and the level of fire protection in a number of towns in Connecticut, including New Haven, and attempts to identify the interactions among fire losses, fire service expenditures, and the ratings assigned towns by the property insurance industry. Despite the simplicity of our methodology and the deficiencies in our data, both these exploratory exercises yield some interesting policy conclusions while suggesting several avenues for future research.

FIRE SERVICES IN NEW HAVEN

The New Haven Fire Department undertakes a number of activities: fire suppression, fire prevention, first aid service, and a number of ancillary activities including training, communication, maintenance, and administration. Fire suppression alone accounts for 88 percent of total employees, and 84 percent of the department budget. Since the ancillary activities primarily support the suppression units, the fire fighting activity dominates the fire budget even more than the fire suppression figures suggest.

The dual objectives of fire services are to limit property damage and prevent casualties due to fires. New Haven averages about 250 fires in buildings per year, although fire fighting units also respond annually to some 400 vehicle fires, 100 false alarms, and 3,000 other calls for service, including trash and brush fires. In administrative practice these nonbuilding fire calls for service appear to have little impact on decisions about levels of fire protection in the city of New Haven. Consequently, our consideration of benefits will focus on fires in buildings. For example, station houses are apparently located to minimize response time to fires in buildings. If station locations were very sensitive to the 400 vehicle fires per year, one might expect closer station proximity to the entrances to the limited access highways servicing New Haven. Similarly, unlike many cities in warmer and drier areas, New Haven faces no serious seasonal problem with brush or forest fires. Such seasonal problems have a significant impact on equipment capacity and labor force decisions.

We also limit our discussion to fire fighting activities. Fire prevention activities[b] may effectively limit the numbers of fires that occur, and may also limit the losses once a fire begins, but our analysis does not attempt to measure or assign these benefits. We might note that

---

[b]Fire prevention activities include inspections of buildings for fire hazards, investigations of fires to identify causes and prosecute arsonists, building plan reviews, and public education.

only 3 percent of the labor force in the New Haven Fire Department is dedicated to fire prevention activities.

Fire-by-Fire Loss Analysis

The first empirical exercise relates losses in building fires to the characteristics of the structures, their occupants, and the neighborhoods in which they are located. To estimate a loss relationship we utilize data on the 256 building fires involving some measurable damage that occurred in New Haven during the year 1972. About 20 percent of these fires involved no pumping activity by the fire department. While some of the "zero pumping" fires were accounted for by fire fighters using dry powder extinguishers to put out electrical fires and by fires in buildings with internal pumping equipment, the primary reason for zero pumping was that the fires were already out when the fire fighters arrived.

Our first question, then, is to ask which fires are likely to involve zero pumping. The results of a simple regression with a dummy dependent variable (1 if no pumping took place, 0 otherwise) and a number of explanatory variables are reported in Table 6-1. (The distortions of statistical tests using a zero/one dependent variable are ignored.) The statistically most significant variable in predicting zero pumping is the value of the building. The more valuable the building where a fire has actually started, the more likely the fire department will pump once it has been called to the scene. High-rise buildings are less likely to require pumping.

There are a number of other significant variables in the equation reported in Table 6-1. Apparently owner-occupants try to put their fires out; fires in nonwooden structures tend to be out when the fire department arrives, and fires in areas with many persons per housing unit tend to be out when the fire fighters arrive. On the other hand, fires in areas with more children, fires in garages and vacant structures, fires caused by careless smokers, and fires of suspicious origin generally require pumping by the fire department.

Given a fire that requires pumping (a "working fire"), we next examine the extent of all property and casualty losses. For working fires Table 6-2 shows the relationship between the proportion of the total structure and contents destroyed and a number of structure and neighborhood variables. The statistically most significant variable in predicting both the proportion of the structure and its contents that will be destroyed by a fire is once again the value of the building. High value buildings tend to lose only a small proportion of their value in a fire. This may be attributable in part to large physical size, more fire resistent construction, the presence of fire walls that confine fire, or more self-protective devices.

Table 6-1. Fire-by-Fire Loss Analysis

Explanatory Variables	Coefficient (t-ratios in parentheses)
Constant term	−1.209
Percent of Census tract population under age 14	−0.008 (2.82)
Height of structure in stories	0.068 (3.61)
Value of the structure (natural log)	−0.085 (5.35)
Percent of the value of the structure loss (natural log)	−0.066 (3.71)
Dummy: 1 if structure contains multiple dwelling units	−0.154 (2.97)
Percent of housing units in Census tract that are owner occupied	0.326 (2.29)
Dummy: 1 if steel or masonry structure	0.101 (1.96)
Dummy: 1 if structure is a garage	−0.235 (2.02)
Persons per housing unit in Census tract	0.041 (1.62)
Dummy: 1 if structure is vacant	−0.081 (1.01)
Dummy: 1 if fire is caused by smoking	−0.086 (1.17)
Dummy: 1 if fire is of suspicious origin	−0.064 (1.05)

Dummy Dependent Variable: 1 = no pumping, 0 = otherwise.
R^2 = 0.24
Number of observations: 256

Fires in garages tend to destroy a larger proportion of their building, as do fires in vacant structures and fires of suspicious origin. Since suspicious fires and fires in vacant buildings are unlikely to be detected until they become large enough to generate smoke visible to passersby, such fires will be hotter when the fire department arrives, and so more difficult to put out; hence, a larger portion of the structure will burn. The higher expected loss rate in black neighborhoods may be the partial result of some reluctance on the part of black residents to call the fire department quickly. We noted above that a fire in an owner occupied building is more likely to be out on the arrival of the fire department; however, the fire damage equation in Table 6-2 shows that a larger portion of the building is likely to be de-

Table 6-2. Fire-by-Fire Loss Analysis—Fire Damage Equation (Working Fires Only)

Explanatory Variables	Coefficient (t-ratios in parentheses)
Constant term	-37.711
Total value of structure and contents (natural log)	-4.460 (5.04)
Dummy: 1 if structure is a garage	12.337 (1.61)
Dummy: 1 if fire is of suspicious origin	4.355 (1.09)
Dummy: 1 if fire is caused by smoking	-6.791 (1.39)
Population per acre	-0.299 (1.64)
Dummy: 1 if structure is vacant	4.565 (0.93)
Percent of Census tract population black	0.023 (0.86)
Median income of families in Census tract	-0.003 (1.60)
Percent of Census tract housing units that are owner occupied	24.828 (1.23)

Dependent Variable: Percent of Value Damaged (0-100 scale).
$R^2 = .45$
Number of observations: 201

stroyed by a working fire in an owner-occupied structure. Overall, those fires likely to be detected and reported quickly, such as fires caused by smokers, fires in densely populated areas, and fires in high income areas, tend to burn a smaller portion of the value of the structure.

As Table 6-3 indicates, casualties (either an injury or a fatality) are likely to occur in residences with more than one unit, in census tracts with a high vacancy rate in the housing stock, and in census tracts with a high rate of substandard housing (as indicated here by incomplete plumbing). Casualties tend to be greater from fires in non-wooden structures and from fires caused by smoking. Casualties are also more likely in census tracts with many persons over age 65. Most casualties are either the aged or children: such persons have more difficulty detecting a fire and more difficulty escaping even if they do detect the danger.

The three equations presented in Tables 6-1, 6-2, and 6-3 describe

Table 6-3. Fire-by-Fire Loss Analysis—Casualty Equation (Working Fires Only)

Explanatory Variables	Coefficient (t-ratios in parentheses)
Constant term	-0.737
Dummy: 1 if structure contains multiple dwelling units	0.092 (0.96)
Percent of housing units in Census tract without plumbing	0.674 (0.75)
Percent of population of Census tract foreign born	-0.048 (2.40)
Percent of population of Census tract aged over 65	0.042 (2.14)
Percent of housing units in Census tract vacant	6.304 (1.92)
Median income of families in Census tract	0.000 (1.22)
Dummy: 1 if fire is caused by smoking	0.107 (0.88)
Dummy: 1 if steel or masonry structure	0.105 (1.15)
Dummy: 1 if residential structure	0.119 (1.06)

Dependent Variable: Number of Casualties
R^2 = .29
Number of observations: 201

the relationships between fire losses and the characteristics of the structures, their occupants, and the neighborhoods in which they are located. We must stress that the above analysis does not account for the quality of the fire department's response. Distance to fire house and response time almost certainly help to explain actual fire loss experience. In order to evaluate properly the quality of the fire department's response, however, it seems crucially important to know the status of the fire upon the arrival of the firefighting crew. Lacking this information we ignore all variables that characterize the quality of the fire department's response.

Conflagrations (fires that spread to other buildings) can be an important source of loss which we have not considered in the above analysis. We chose to ignore conflagrations both due to the complexity of the problem and the lack of relevant data. Of 1,236 building fires in New Haven during a five-year period, only 26 involved more than one structure, and only nine involved more than two.

Identifying the Beneficiaries of Fire Services

To measure benefits and assign them to classes of property owners, we employ a "counterfactual" approach. We first make an assumption regarding the size of the loss that would occur if a fire broke out in a structure and no fire department responded. Benefits are then equal to the expected loss in this obviously counterfactual circumstance, less the expected fire loss when a fire department does, indeed, respond to the fire. Since we are examining only fire suppression activity, we ignore the impact of a fire department in preventing fires; i.e., we assume that the probability of a fire's breaking out is unaffected by the existence of a fire fighting response. Since we do not have information on losses in any city that had no fire fighting response, we make a number of different counterfactual assumptions.

We attempt to evaluate both property and casualty losses. The fire marshall's estimates of the dollar value of loss is our measure of damages in the presence of fire fighting. We define three situations to measure property damages in the absence of fire fighting. The first situation (Assumption I) assumes that the entire structure and all its contents are destroyed every time there is a fire; the second situation (Assumption II) assumes that some fraction of the structure and its contents are destroyed; and the third situation (Assumption III) assumes that damages are related to various structural and neighborhood characteristics.

We use actual casualties reported by the fire marshall as our estimate of casualties that occur in the presence of the fire department. Our counterfactual assumption about casualties (Assumption IV) in the absence of a fire fighting effort is that every time an actual casualty occurs in the presence of a fire fighting response, all the occupants of the structure would have died had the fire department not responded.

Presumably, we can estimate an expected loss in the absence of a fire fighting response and an expected loss in the presence of a fire fighting response for each structure. The difference seems to be the value of the fire fighting response to that structure and its occupants. In Tables 6-4, 6-5, 6-6, and 6-7, we estimate the value of fire fighting to different classes of structures under these various assumptions. Such a value might serve as a basis for a fire fighting user charge. One way in which a user charge might be calculated would be to apportion the total *value* of fire fighting services to individual structures, taking into account structural characteristics, private extinguishers, smoke detectors, and the like. The fire fighting value, or some fixed fraction, might be collected as a fire service charge. The total revenue collected by the fire service would aid the public agency in determining the desired level of public fire fighting activity, while at the same time the user charge would encourage individuals to undertake fire protection measures privately.

Assumption I is the simplest. According to this assumption, every time there is a fire the entire building would burn if the fire fighters did not respond; hence, the difference between the total value of each building where a fire occurred and the actual damage experienced is the benefit attributable to the fire fighting activity. The value of fire fighting to different structural classes under this scheme is shown in Table 6-4.

According to this assumption, the total benefit from fire fighting in New Haven from 1968 through 1972 was $62.6 million annually. Over 39 percent of these benefits were assigned to nonresidential occupancies. Although taxed property represents over two-thirds of total property value, it received only 50 percent of the benefits from fire protection. Yale University alone enjoyed over 35 percent and the city government over 12 percent of the total value of fire fighting under Assumption I.

A simple alternative, and perhaps more plausible counterfactual assumption—although no less arbitrary—is that the loss rate for any fire in the absence of the fire department is simply double what it is in the presence of the fire department (up to 100 percent maximum loss). Under this Assumption II, the total benefits are $11.1 million annually (see Table 6-5). Under this scheme, 64 percent of the bene fits are assigned to nonresidential use, 66 percent to taxed property and over 15 percent to Yale.

The difference in the pattern of property benefits between Table 6-4 and Table 6-5 is substantial. Under the first scheme, small damage fires in high value buildings attribute very substantial benefits to buildings that have small fires. Under the second scheme, the value of the buildings where fires occur has little impact on total benefits. Consequently, the proportion of benefits accruing to different property groups shifts considerably. Clearly, the allocation of benefits is quite sensitive to the choice of counterfactual assumptions.

Making use of our estimated equation on fire losses, we can adjust the expected losses in the absence of fire fighting for the probability that a fire is out on arrival; that is, for any structure, the probability of a working fire's breaking out is reduced by an amount appropriate to that structure. Furthermore, we can make use of our information about fire damages for different structural classes in the presence of the fire department to modify our estimate of expected losses in the

Table 6-4. Benefit Calculations With Counterfactual Assumption I, New Haven 1968-1972—Benefits to Property Assuming Total Structure Loss for Every Fire (thousands of dollars)

		Residential Uses							
Ownership	Nonresidential Uses	Owner Occupied	Tenant Occupied	Hospital	College Dorm	Public Housing	Vacant	Hotel	Totals
Individual	13,483	6,129	22,637	0	171	0	2,451	158	45,029 (14.4)[a]
Corporate	72,315	182	19,106	1,948	0	0	393	17,079	111,023 (35.5)
Yale University	22,502	0	0	0	88,150	0	0	0	110,652 (35.4)
Churches	407	0	0	0	0	0	0	0	407 (0.1)
City government	10,418	0	0	0	0	28,323	180	16	38,937 (12.4)
State government	1,847	0	0	0	0	2,161	0	0	4,008 (1.3)
Federal government	999	0	0	0	0	0	0	0	999 (0.3)
Penn Central Railroad	15	0	0	0	0	0	0	0	15 (0.0)
Other tax-exempt properties	1,568	0	0	0	17	174	34	0	1,793 (0.6)
Column total	123,554 (39.5)	6,311 (2.0)	41,743 (13.4)	1,948 (0.6)	88,338 (28.2)	30,658 (9.8)	3,058 (1.0)	17,253 (5.5)	312,863 (100.0)

[a]Percent of total benefits in parentheses.

Table 6-5. Benefit Calculations with Counterfactual Assumption II, New Haven 1968-1972—Benefits to Property Assuming Total Structure Loss for Every Fire (thousands of dollars)

Ownership	Nonresidential Uses	Residential Uses							Totals
		Owner Occupied	Tenant Occupied	Hospital	College Dorm	Public Housing	Vacant	Hotel	
Individual	4,981	1,575	4,667	0	60	0	1,034	38	12,355 (22.3)[a]
Corporate	19,855	49	2,251	129	0	0	203	1,603	24,090 (43.4)
Yale University	6,041	0	0	0	2,529	0	0	0	8,570 (15.5)
Churches	249	0	0	0	0	0	0	0	249 (0.4)
City government	3,153	0	0	0	0	5,196	83	7	8,439 (15.2)
State government	361	0	0	0	0	426	0	0	787 (1.4)
Federal government	389	0	0	0	0	0	0	0	389 (0.7)
Penn Central Railroad	7	0	0	0	0	0	0	0	7 (0.0)
Other tax-exempt properties	556	0	0	0	1	31	15	0	603 (1.1)
Column total	35,592 (64.1)	1,624 (2.9)	6,918 (12.5)	129 (0.2)	2,590 (4.7)	5,653 (10.2)	1,335 (2.4)	1,648 (3.0)	55,489 (100.0)

[a]Percent of total benefits in parentheses.

absence of a fire department response. For example, we know that garage fires tend to destroy a large proportion of the structure. Thus, in the event of a garage fire without fire fighting response, we assume that a larger than average proportion will burn.

Operationally, to modify loss expectations for structure and neighborhood characteristics we modify the constant term in the loss equation reported in Table 6-2 for substitution into the equation of the mean values of all the independent variables to yield a predicted loss of 100 percent. We then calculate an expected loss in the absence of a fire fighting response using the new constant term and the actual structure and neighborhood variables. The maximum loss permitted is 100 percent. Note that we use the loss equation for working fires only; fires that are out on arrival yield no benefits under Assumption III.

The modification of loss expectations for structural characteristics may not go far enough. Buidings can be constructed so that fire barriers (e.g., fire walls) limit the extent of fire loss to some portion of the building under all but extraordinary circumstances. The spread of a fire from one zone to another within a large structure is similar to a conflagration between detached buildings. Assumption III, therefore, treats "fire zones" within large buildings as distinct units and assumes that the 100 percent loss is restricted to the fire unit. Losses due to fire spreading beyond the units—i.e, conflagration—are ignored. Unfortunately, available data do not allow us to define fire zones explicitly. Consequently, our simplistic fire zone adjustment assumes that all fires occur in fire zones with an estimated value of $250,000, or the actual total value of the structure, whichever is less. The net effect of this assumption is that the maximum loss in the absence of a fire fighting response is $250,000.

Table 6-6 gives the breakdown of benefits by property classes under Assumption III. The total benefit is $12 million annually. Under this set of assumptions, 71 percent of the benefits accrue to taxed properties, almost 38 percent to non-residential properties, and 10.5 percent to city-owned structures (including 7.6 percent to city-owned public housing).

In addition to reducing property losses, there are benefits from reduction in casualties due to fire fighting activity. According to counterfactual Assumption IV, if there is at least one casualty with fire fighting, then in the absence of fire fighting all occupants would have been fatalities. The number of occupants in the structure is assumed equal to the average number of occupants per dwelling in the census tract in which the fire is located. When an injury occurs, we assume that the fire service prevented a death.

Table 6-6. Benefit Calculations with Counterfactual Assumption III, New Haven 1968-1972—Benefits to Property Adjusted for Out-on-Arrival Fires, Structure Characteristics and Fire Units (thousands of dollars)

Ownership	Nonresidential Uses	Residential Uses							Totals
		Owner Occupied	Tenant Occupied	Hospital	College Dorm	Public Housing	Vacant	Hotel	
Individual	8,609	3,944	13,018	0	144	0	1,908	129	27,752 (46.4)[a]
Corporate	8,511	125	3,504	248	0	0	364	2,059	14,811 (24.8)
Yale University	2,497	0	0	0	6,368	0	0	0	8,865 (14.8)
Churches	313	0	0	0	0	0	0	0	313 (0.5)
City government	1,530	0	0	0	0	4,549	171	8	6,258 (10.5)
State government	543	0	0	0	0	543	0	0	1,086 (1.8)
Federal government	249	0	0	0	0	0	0	0	249 (0.4)
Penn Central Railroad	10	0	0	0	0	0	0	0	10 (0.0)
Other tax-exempt properties	318	0	0	0	13	110	34	0	475 (0.8)
Column total	22,580 (37.7)	4,069 (6.8)	16,522 (26.5)	248 (0.4)	6,525 (10.9)	5,202 (8.7)	2,477 (4.1)	2,196 (3.7)	59,819 (100.0)

[a]Percent of total benefits in parentheses.

Table 6–7 shows the benefits due to reductions in fatalities for a five-year period in New Haven, when the value of a life saved is $200,000.[c] The total value of lives saved under this calculation is $10.9 million annually. Of this amount, 82 percent is attributed to residential fires and 18 percent to nonresidential fires. Of the casualty benefit, over 85 percent is attributed to individuals and corporations which are taxable, and almost 15 percent to various tax-exempt properties (5.5 percent of the casualty benefit accrues to Yale University).

The total benefit of the fire fighting activity is the sum of the benefits due to reduction in property and casualty losses. Using the property loss savings calculated under Assumption III and the casualty loss savings just presented (Assumption IV), the total benefit of fire fighting in New Haven is $22.8 million per year. The total cost of operating the fire department on an annual basis, including capital costs, is about $6.7 million. Thus, the aggregate average benefit-cost ratio is over three. (This estimate is obviously quite sensitive to the accuracy of the benefit measurement procedures.)

These benefit and cost measures account for the total fire fighting activity and the total benefits derived, and thus do not bear on the question of whether the size of the fire department should be changed.

To determine the optimal size of a fire department, information about the incremental benefits associated with marginal changes in fire fighting activity is necessary. This is the subject of the next section where we examine fire damages and fire fighting expenditures across a sample of Connecticut communities.

FIRE EXPENDITURES, LOSSES, AND INSURANCE RATINGS IN CONNECTICUT TOWNS

Obviously, a major objective of fire fighting expenditures is to reduce property losses due to fire. A secondary objective of fire fighting expenditures, however, may be to achieve a particular rating with the property insurance industry, since a better rating brings lower insurance premiums for town residents. Therefore, we now examine the relationship between insurance ratings and fire fighting expenditures, as well as the relationship between property losses and expenditures on fire fighting.

Although not entirely suited to the purpose, we utilize levels of actual losses as our measure of the output of fire fighting activities. If

[c]This is an arbitrary value approximately equal to the present discounted value of a lifetime earnings stream.

Table 6-7. Benefit Calculations with Counterfactual Assumption IV, New Haven 1968–1972—Benefits to Life Not Adjusted for Out-on-Arrival (thousands of dollars)

Ownership	Nonresidential Uses	Owner Occupied	Tenant Occupied	Hospital	College Dorm	Public Housing	Vacant	Hotel	Totals
		Residential Uses							
Individual	5,466	10,396	23,415	50	106	46	914	457	40,850 (74.8)[a]
Corporate	3,142	209	1,409	62	0	0	180	498	5,500 (10.1)
Yale University	745	0	0	0	2,257	0	0	0	3,002 (5.5)
Churches	1	0	0	0	0	0	0	0	1 (0.0)
City government	288	0	0	0	0	3,764	134	27	4,213 (7.7)
State government	113	0	0	0	0	524	42	0	679 (1.2)
Federal government	13	0	0	0	0	0	0	0	13 (0.0)
Penn Central Railroad	228	0	0	0	0	0	0	0	228 (0.4)
Other tax-exempt properties	37	0	0	0	79	12	10	0	138 (0.3)
Column total	10,033 (18.4)	10,605 (19.4)	24,824 (45.4)	112 (0.2)	2,442 (4.5)	4,346 (8.0)	1,280 (2.3)	982 (1.8)	54,624 (100.0)

[a]Percent of total benefits in parentheses.

differences in hazard are not taken into account, then when actual fire losses are used as a measure of output, an anomaly may result: increases in fire losses will occur with increases in expenditures on fire services. Thus the high hazard localities may have the largest fire service expenditures and the largest actual losses.

We attempt to solve this problem in two ways. First, we explicitly include in the model a substantial number of variables that may relate to hazard: total property value, proportion of total assessed value that is in dwellings, the proportion of housing units that are vacant, crowded, and densely occupied; the proportion of families who are poor, the proportions of the population that are young and old; the number of high rise structures; the proportion of structures that are old; the proportion of housing units heated by oil; population density; and structural density. Census data and local government audit reports are used to measure these variables. Unfortunately, data on types of construction, and on the character of industrial and commercial occupancies, are not readily available. It could be argued that the number of fires breaking out is a measure of hazard and is little affected by fire service activity. To the extent that fire prevention activities are effective and vary over space, this argument is not correct.

As in our analysis of the New Haven fire experience, there is an even more serious problem in measuring the output of fire fighting activity related to casualty losses. In addition to the problem of estimating the value of a human life, there is the problem of quantifying the value of physical impairments. This valuation problem is critical because changes in fire fighting behavior may transform statistical deaths into statistical injuries. Because of these problems and the simplistic nature of our own loss model, we chose to ignore casualty losses.

The Loss Equation

Losses will vary depending upon the level of fire service expenditures. The relationship is largely a technological one. Additional expenditures buy additional equipment, more station houses, and pay the salaries of additional fire fighters. Increased fire fighting effort can be applied in various ways to reduce losses due to fire.[1]

The relationship between losses and expenditures will depend heavily upon the availability of water. Large water mains, which can carry enough water for fire fighting, are common in areas with sewers. Census information on the proportion of housing units supplied by water mains and served by sewer lines are included in the model.

The larger the area served by a fire department, other things equal, the greater the response time and the larger the losses. But large departments can organize backup support more easily. The loss equation, therefore, relates a variable measuring the loss per fire (the output measure) to the level of local expenditures, the characteristics of the water system, the area of the locality, and the set of hazard-related variables.

The Insurance Rating

The fire insurance industry greatly influences the supply of local fire services. The insurance industry grades each municipality on a scale from one to ten, and fire insurance rates are tied to the rating: the lower the grade, the lower the premiums on fire insurance. In determining the rating for the municipality, the insurance organization assigns "deficiency points" in each of four categories. The maximum deficiency scores that can be assigned in each category are: water, 1,950; fire department, 1,950; communications, 450; and fire safety control, 650.[2] The grading is determined by a periodic (every ten to twenty years) survey by engineers from the Insurance Service Office (ISO) regional offices.

Localities will not significantly modify their fire service activity without consulting ISO and determining the impact of the change on their insurance grade. Any change that will threaten to increase the number of deficiency points is unlikely to be implemented. On the other hand, the insurance industry continually maintains pressure on the localities to increase the level of their fire service activity. Since there is a lag between premium adjustments and actual loss experience, the insurance industry may derive an actuarial gain with each improvement in fire service.

The second relation of the model describes the assignment of deficiency scores by the insurance industry.[d] The principal explanatory variables are the level of fire service expenditures, the water and area variables, and the set of variables that relate to hazard.

The Expenditure Decision

Municipalities determine the level of fire service expenditures as a part of their budgetary process. The number of competing goods that must be financed from local sources influences the amount allocated to fire fighting. The size of the tax base as measured by income (percent of families who are poor, in this formulation), the market value of property, and the taxes collected per person (net of fire ex-

[d]The Insurance Service Office supplied the rating for each municipality—one to ten—and indicated whether the municipality scored above or below the middle of its rating class. From this information an estimate of the total deficiency score for each municipality was made.

penditure), are each included as measures of fiscal constraints. The loss experience of the town, as well as other variables relating to the degree of hazard, are included here because they determine potential willingness to spend for fire fighting service.

The Results

The model outlined above consists of three equations, three endogenous variables, and seventeen exogenous variables. The variables are described in Table 6-8. The model was estimated using two-stage least squares estimation techniques and data for 31 towns in Connecticut with some paid fire fighters. The results of the estimation are presented in Table 6-9. The explanatory power of the insurance rating equation is reasonably satisfactory. The adjusted R^2 of .65 indicates that the regression explains a significant portion of the variation in deficiency point scores.

However, the only statistically significant coefficient in the deficiency point equation is the proportion of housing units served by sewer lines. The negative sign is expected: where there are sewers, there are usually larger water mains with fire fighting capacity. The insurance industry seems to weight heavily the presence of substantial water carrying capacity. A percentage point increase in the proportion of housing units sewered (large water mains) will lower the deficiency score by 28 points. The positive sign on the water main variable would seem to indicate that a municipality is penalized in its fire grade by housing units that are served by water mains but lack sewers, for such water mains are probably of small capacity.

The fact that all the other variables in the insurance rating equation are not significantly different from zero is a likely consequence of the multicolinearity among many of the variables. One might exclude some variables or use the technique of principal components to increase the statistical power of the estimation. It is worth noting, however, that despite the lack of statistical significance, most variables have the anticipated signs. The most noticeable exception is the expenditures variable, which has an unanticipated negative sign.

The results of the estimation of the second equation of the model, the expenditure relation, are also reported in Table 6-9. Local government expenditures are explained by the loss experience, fiscal capacity, and the degree of hazard. The explanatory power of the equation is substantial, with an adjusted R^2 of .93.

Structural density and the proportion of the housing stock that is in the high rise structures have positive coefficients that are significantly different from zero. The coefficients of old structures and population density also have positive signs, and are close to being sig-

Table 6-8. Fire Expenditures, Losses, and Insurance Ratings—List of Variables for Three-Equation Models

Endogenous

1. Losses   Average loss per fire in 1972.

2. Expenditures   Local government expenditures on the fire service in 1972 in $10,000 units.

3. Deficiency   The estimated number of deficiency points assigned to the municipality by the Insurance Service Office.

Exogenous

1. Water   The proportion of housing units served by water mains, 1970 Census.

2. Sewer   The proportion of housing units served by sewer lines, 1970 Census.

3. Area   Area in the town in square miles.

4. True value   The market value of taxable property in the town: the assessed value divided by the statutory assessment ratio, 1972.

5. Taxes   Property tax collections less fire service expenditures per capita, 1972 taxes, 1970 population.

6. Structural density   Number of housing structures per total acreage, 1970 Census.

7. Old structures   The proportion of housing structures built before 1940, 1970 Census.

8. Population density   Population per acre, 1970 Census.

9. High rise   The proportion of housing units in buildings over four stories tall.

10. Oil heat   The proportion of housing units heated by oil.

11. Residential   The proportion of total property assessments accounted for by residences.

12. Owner-occupied   The proportion of housing units that are owner-occupied.

13. Vacant   The proportion of housing units that are vacant.

14. Crowded   The proportion of occupied housing units with more than one person per room.

15. Poor   The proportion of families with income below the poverty line, 1970.

16. Under 5   The proportion of population aged 5 or less.

17. Over 65   The proportion of the population aged 65 or more.

Table 6-9. Fire Loss and Expenditure in Connecticut Towns

Explanatory Variables	Deficiency Points	Expenditures (t-ratios in parentheses)	Loss
Constant	798.323 (0.12)	−446.067 (−0.92)	.416 (0.00)
$ Loss per fire	—	.844 (0.23)	—
Expenditures on fire	−4.421 (−0.29)	—	−0.161 (−0.36)
% Housing with water mains	11.270 (1.13)	—	.404 (1.39)
% Housing sewered	−28.103 (−2.58)	—	−0.343 (−1.17)
Area	6.706 (0.77)	.700 (1.03)	.101 (0.40)
True value	−0.022 (−0.30)	−0.005 (−0.86)	−0.001 (−0.67)
Taxes	—	1.813 (0.41)	—
Structural density	1.310 (0.03)	2.555 (3.12)	.410 (0.35)
% Housing that is old structures	13.029 (0.22)	3.602 (1.29)	−0.147 (−0.08)
Population density	77.220 (0.71)	7.509 (1.48)	.857 (0.27)
% Housing high-rise	1.218 (0.15)	.442 (2.08)	.063 (0.27)
% Housing oil heat	3.324 (0.17)	1.028 (0.54)	.018 (0.03)
% Assessed value residential	−0.008 (0.00)	−0.003 (−0.01)	−0.004 (−0.08)
% Housing owner-occupied	.162 (0.00)	2.098 (0.84)	−0.472 (−0.38)
% Housing vacant	−66.931 (−0.66)	4.597 (0.67)	2.107 (0.72)
% Housing crowded	64.414 (0.62)	10.373 (0.56)	1.310 (0.43)
% Population poor	−52.570 (−0.23)	13.593 (1.67)	.678 (0.10)
% Population under five	49.425 (0.40)	−1.677 (−0.12)	−0.111 (−0.03)
% Population over 65	96.404 (0.39)	−10.912 (−0.77)	2.063 (0.29)
Adjusted R^2:	.65	.93	.66

Number of observations: 31

nificant by usual standards. This set of variables suggests that there is a greater willingness to spend for fire services in old, dense cities. Perhaps the public senses the possibility of conflagration, or perhaps the older structures create a greater awareness of the fire hazard.

The model's loss equation (also reported in Table 6-9) is the relation with the greatest policy signficance. Here inputs—local government fire expenditures—are directly related to outputs—losses per fire. Expenditure levels, loss experience, and the insurance rating are jointly determined. The regression results are very weak: the unadjusted R^2 is only .28. None of the coefficients is significantly different from zero, although lack of significance may be partly the result of multicolinearity. The signs of the coefficients are typically as expected.

SUMMARY

The obvious limitations of the analysis we have just presented clearly indicates that our understanding of the forces that shape fire service delivery is still quite primitive. Despite this primitive understanding, however, we can make several important observations from our exploratory analysis.

First, the city itself, particularly its public housing activities, is apparently a major beneficiary of fire fighting services. This implies that capital investment decisions in the public sector ought to include these service costs in the decision-making calculus. Similarly, payment-in-lieu-of-tax schemes from higher to lower levels of government might reflect the fire service benefit to govenment properties. It should similarly be acknowledged that to the extent that tax-exempt properties consume local fire services for which they might be expected to pay, charges proportional to property value may not be an entirely satisfactory basis for the charge. Occupancy and self-protection efforts, at a minimum, should also be taken into account.

A second conclusion is that although we may not yet be sophisticated enough to fully allocate fire fighting costs to beneficiaries, it is quite clear that property use, maintenance levels, vacancy rates, and self-protection measures are important factors affecting the level of demand placed on the municipal fire service. Small marginal charges might well be levied based upon this knowledge. Such charges (or discounts) would provide a valuable incentive for self-protection. Candidates for discounts would include buildings with sprinklers, owner-occupied housing units, and masonry structures. Candidates for surcharge would be garages and vacant units.

The importance of neighborhood and property value variables in determining fire losses indicates that the property tax provides a disincentive, on the margin, for private fire protection. Neighborhood variables usually associated with higher property values (and, hence, higher taxes) often reduce fire loss; self-protection devices increase the value of a property and reduce the risk of fire. Yet in both cases, reduced risk of fire loss is associated with higher charges to support the fire service activity.

A third conclusion is that smoking is a significant cause of fire. This might imply that even heavier cigarette taxation is called for, with some of the revenue earmarked for fire protection.

Clearly the empirical evidence we have examined, although quite incomplete, does suggest some possible policy experiments. For example, what would be the reduction in fire losses associated with the widespread availability of home fire extinguishers or smoke detectors? One could envision, say, a biannual purchase of fire extinguishers for residential dwellings, the cost being directly offset by a reduction in the property tax bill.

Since fire insurance premiums are not simply based on the value of a structure, but rather are differentiated with respect to structural characteristics and self-protective measures, perhaps a fire service user charge can be based on fire insurance premiums. A proportional excise tax on fire insurance premiums might have the desirable effect of giving incentives for more self-protective measures. An excise with different rates in different towns might have the effect of making the fire service more cost conscious. It may also be possible to permit some specific credits for private fire protection measures. A reduction in insurance premium might be allowed, for example, if a smoke detector or extinquisher were in place. Fire service user charges tied to fire insurance premiums appear to have considerable promise.

The inadequate explanatory power of the fire department expenditure variables in the cross-sectional analysis of fire losses suggests we are far from the day when we can use such analysis to determine the optimal level of local fire protection. The absence of a relation, however, should constitute a warning to local decision makers: in order to reduce fire losses, attention must be given to several considerations—including land use, the water supply, and fire prevention—as well as fire fighting.

Chapter 7

Police Services—Their Costs and Financing

Peter Kemper
Roger W. Schmenner

In recent years, the resources that local governments have devoted to police services have increased at a rapid rate.

Nationwide during the period 1957 to 1971, the number of policemen increased by 67 percent and total expenditures on police increased by 142 percent.[1] Measured in constant 1967 dollars, per capita police expenditures have doubled, from $9 in 1957 to about $18 in 1971. At the same time, crime rates have soared, growing 151 percent between 1960 and 1972.[2] These high rates of growth have repeatedly focused public attention on the delivery of police services. The research reported here asks a number of questions about police services: What are the types of police services now provided? What is the cost of each of these services? Who consumes them? Where are they consumed? How can they best be financed?

This paper is divided into two distinct parts. The first is a positive analysis of the costs of providing police services. The second is a normative discussion of financing these services through special charges. The first part begins with a description of the many different responsibilities of the police and then uses data from Bridgeport, Connecticut, to estimate the costs of providing particular kinds of service. These estimates, which are based on the amount of time the police spend responding to each type of call for service, provide answers to the questions about the type and cost of specific police services.

The second part, that dealing with financing, begins with a distinction between "user charges" and "class charges" and a discussion of the efficiency of these charges for five major categories of police service. Empirical estimates of the incidence of police expenditures by income class in Bridgeport are then presented. An assessment of special charges for police services concludes Part II. The paper concludes with a brief summary.

PART I THE COST OF POLICE SERVICES

The Bridgeport Police Department, serving a predominantly industrial city of 150,000 inhabitants, provided us with detailed information on expenses and personnel assignments. The data not only identified the functions a police department is called on to perform, but they also indicated which functions demanded relatively more resources than others.

The Nature of Police Services

Most city police departments are complex organizations, and the police department of the city of Bridgeport is no exception. The Bridgeport police number about 445, 16 percent in supervisory work (superintendent, inspectors, captains, lieutenants, and sergeants) and the rest in patrolman and technician positions. They serve in ten divisions, as shown in Table 7-1. These divisions within Bridgeport's police department perform a wide variety of functions.

Patrol. Police patrol activities engage the bulk (54 percent) of police manpower. Platoons within the patrol division are typically set up to provide routine round-the-clock surveillance by car, and day and evening surveillance by foot. Police from the patrol division are generally the first to react to citizen calls for service, although police from other divisions may follow up these calls with additional service. Calls for service may range from the rendering of medical assistance or the investigation of a motor vehicle accident to arrests made vice charges or the handling of a family dispute.

Detective. Although police patrols may begin investigations of crimes, these investigations are usually carried through by the detective division of the department. Although the detective division initiates some investigations on their own, most investigations grow out of the calls initially handled by the patrol division.

Traffic. All direction of traffic and parking law enforcement, and many of the city's motor vehicle violations, are handled by the traffic division of the department. This division also is responsible for maintaining traffic signals and parking meters throughout the city.

Table 7-1. Manpower Chart of the Bridgeport Police Department

Category	Supervisory Personnel[a]	Patrolmen, Detectives, Technicians	Patrolman Equivalents[b]	Patrolmen Equivalent as % of Total
I. Administration	11	40	58.09	11.9%
Executive Office	3	1	7.50	1.5%
Records	3	21	25.26	5.2%
Clerical	2	1	3.77	0.8%
Planning & Operations	3	17	21.56	4.4%
II. Patrol	36	204	253.86	52.0%
III. Traffic	5	43	50.03	10.3%
IV. Detective	8	29	46.76	9.6%
V. Special Duty Services	7	46	60.63	12.4%
Tactical & K-9	3	23	27.08	5.6%
Special Services	2	10	14.85	3.0%
Youth Bureau	2	13	18.70	3.8%
VI. Training and Relief	6	6	15.50	3.2%
Relief	4	—	6.73	1.4%
Training & Community Relations	2	6	8.77	1.8%
VII. Mechanical Division	—	3	3	0.6%
Total	73	371	487.87	100.0%

[a]Includes superintendent, inspectors, captains, lieutenants, and sergeants.
[b]"Patrolman equivalents" are calculated according to the base salary received.

Tactical, Special Services, and Youth. Riots, narcotics, vice, juvenile crime, and large-scale department mobilizations are the responsibilities of these divisions of the department.

Administration, Mechanical, and Training. A substantial number of people are required to manage the department, to plan and evaluate its operations, to maintain its records, to oversee its vehicles, and to train its people.

From a Line Item to a Program Budget

Estimating the average cost of each of the services provided by these divisions is not a simple task. Because city budgets are oriented toward types of expenditures rather than types of services provided, a considerable amount of work is necessary to estimate specific service costs from budget data. Figure 7-1 illustrates the task of transforming a "line item budget" into a "program budget." The left-hand block represents the total cost incurred by the police department broken down by type of expense as it appears in the city budget. The right-hand block represents the program budget, which reflects the same total cost broken down by type of service. Constructing the program budget consists of three main tasks: (1) adjusting the police budget by adding any omitted costs so that the budget reflects the full economic cost of providing police services; (2) allocating the full cost of police to the various divisions within the department; and (3) allocating the costs incurred by each division to the specific types of services they provide.

The principles we have used to estimate the average cost of specific types of service are quite simple. The cost of those resources that are clearly used to perform only one type of service are attributed to that type of service. The costs of those resources that perform more than one function are allocated to separate services according to the amount of time spent on each service (as explained in detail below). Together these two types of cost constitute total direct cost.

The remaining indirect costs cannot be attributed directly to a particular service because they are inputs into joint production; they are allocated to services on an arbitrary but reasonable basis (as explained below). The resulting estimates of cost of specific services are therefore approximations of the average cost of providing that service. The marginal cost of providing many services is undoubtedly less than this average cost, especially in the short run, but we have made no effort to estimate marginal cost. What follows is a rather detailed discussion of the cost estimation procedures. Readers who are interested only in the results may wish to examine Figure 7-1 and then skip to the section titled "Results."

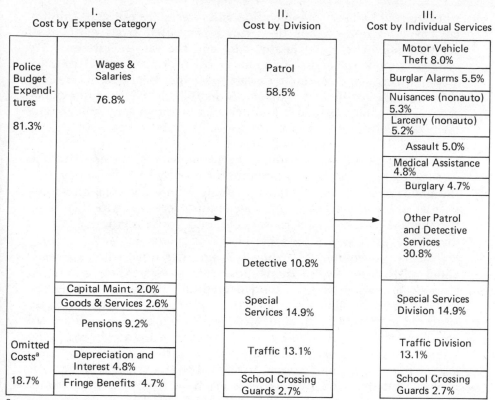

Figure 7-1. Procedure for Estimating Costs for Individual Police Services

Adding Omitted Costs. Adjusting the police budget to represent the full economic cost of providing police services is relatively straightforward. While the line item current fund budget includes direct wages and salaries, expenses for the maintenance and operation of capital equipment, and the cost of goods and services purchased, it does not include the police department's share of the city's expenditures on fringe benefits and pensions, depreciation, or interest. These costs must be estimated and included in the total cost.

The cost of fringe benefits is approximately 6.5 percent of wages and salaries.[a] Police pension payments appear as a separate item else-

---

[a] The 6.5 percent figure is computed from Table 7-2 as line IIA divided by line IC3. The fringe benefits cited are the police department's allocated share (by payroll) of the city's expenditures for employee maintenance (Title 11-Series 115 of the City Budget), including social security, health and life insurance, and some other more minor expenses.

where in the budget.b Depreciation and interest do not appear in the current fund budget, but they can be imputed from the cost of capital equipment, its estimated life, and the rate of interest. City officials supplied the first two pieces of information, and we have arbitrarily assumed an interest rate of 8 percent.c As Table 7-2 shows, the police budget understates the full cost of providing police services by about 19 percent. Much of this rather large understatement results from the omission of fringe benefits and pensions.

Estimating Cost by Division.   The second step in the construction of the program budget is to estimate the cost by each division within the police department. We have combined these divisions into four: patrol, traffic,d detective, and special duty services (which includes the tactical and K-9, special services, and youth divisions). A fifth division is comprised of the school crossing guards.

The second column of Table 7-2 indicates how each expense is allocated to these five divisions. Some expenses are clearly incurred by a single division and can be allocated directly to it; for example, the cost of maintaining traffic lights and parking meters is directly allocated to the traffic division. Most expenses, however, are incurred for resources that are used by all divisions. For example, wages and salaries are paid to patrolmen who work in different divisions. These labor expenses, including costs attributed to training and relief, have been allocated to the five divisions in proportion to the manpower devoted to each, as was shown in Table 7-1. Capital expenses, including the costs attributed to the mechanical division, are similarly allocated in proportion to the value of equipment used by each division, as shown in Table 7-3. After the labor and the capital expenses are allocated to divisions, overhead (administrative) expenses are allocated in proportion to total expenses (other than overhead).

The estimates of expenses by division resulting from these various allocations are shown in Table 7-4. Approximately 60 percent of the total cost of police services is incurred by the patrol division; 15 per-

bThe actual pension expenditures are for patrolmen who have already retired. Since the police department has grown, future pension expenses will greatly exceed the current pension expenses. A better estimate would require inputting the premium that would be required to fund the retirement benefits guaranteed to the present police force. We have contented ourselves with the more easily estimated current pension expenses.

cThe cost of services provided to the police department by other city agencies should also be included in total police costs. Because estimating these costs would be expensive, and because they are undoubtedly small, we have chosen to ignore them.

dIncluded in the traffic division cost is the cost of maintaining the police boat.

Table 7-2. Police Costs, by Type of Expense, 1972-1973

Type of Expense	How Allocated to Divisions	Cost	% of Total Police Service Costs
I. Police Budget Expenditures		$6,203,736	81.3%
A. Goods and Services		194,770	2.6%
1. Supplies	By total other expenses	12,608	0.2%
2. Postage, Telephone and Supplies	"	18,313	0.2%
3. Legal & Auxiliary Services	"	4,389	0.1%
4. Subsistence & Care	To special services division	47,385	0.6%
5. Police Training, Books & Tuition	By labor expenses	4,882	0.1%
6. Uniforms, Badges & Identification	"	107,193	1.4%
B. Capital Equipment, Maintenance and Operation		150,088	2.0%
1. Building Maintenance	By total expenses	9,785	0.1%
2. Heat & Utilities	"	33,363	0.5%
3. Vehicle Maintenance	By value of vehicle	34,251	0.5%
4. Accidental Damage	"	49	0.0%
5. Gasoline	"	26,033	0.3%
6. Traffic Light & Parking meter maintenance	To traffic division	44,720	0.6%
7. Boat maintenance	"	1,887	0.0%
C. Wages and Salaries		5,858,878	76.8%
1. School Guards	By total other expenses	152,027	2.0%
2. Clerical & Custodial	By labor expenses	164,198	2.2%
3. Patrolmen & Officers	"	5,542,653	72.6%
II. Costs Not Included in Budget		$1,426,276	18.7%
A. Fringe Benefits	By labor expenses	357,516	4.7%
B. Pensions	"	700,440	9.2%
C. Depreciation & Interest	"	368,320	4.8%
1. Buildings	By total other expenses	275,000	2.6%
2. Sedans	By value of vehicle	47,755	0.6%
3. Wagons & Vans	"	14,400	0.2%
4. Trucks	"	13,035	0.2%
5. Motorcycles	"	18,130	0.2%
Total Costs for Police Services		$7,630,012	100.0%

Source: Annual Audit Report as of June 30, 1973, City of Bridgeport, Connecticut.

cent by the special services divisions; 13 percent by the traffic division; 11 percent by the detective division; and 3 percent by the school crossing guards.

Estimating Cost by Type of Service. The final step in estimating the cost of each type of service is to allocate these division expenses to the specific services provided. For some of the divisions this is not possible. For example, the traffic division provides several unique services with wide-ranging benefits, but the data needed to break down traffic division expenses into more specific categories are not available. Such traffic expenses are simply lumped together as if only one service were provided by the division. However, for the patrol and detective divisions, the allocation of police division expenses to specific services is possible but difficult.

In the patrol division, cars are assigned to specific areas or "beats" within the city. During its shift, a patrol car is responsible for the sur-

Table 7-3. Capital Equipment

Category	Number	Depreciation & Interest	% of Total
1. Administrative		$3,660	4.0
Sedans	2	2,750	
Vans	1	910	
2. Patrol		29,190	31.7
Sedans	18	23,430	
Wagons and Vans	4	5,760	
3. Traffic		32,970	35.8
Sedans	3	4,130	
Wagons and Vans	2	2,880	
Trucks	9	12,630	
Motorcycles	19	18,130	
4. Detective			
Sedans	4	5,510	6.0
5. Special duty services		12,580	13.7
Sedans	6	8,260	
Wagons	3	4,320	
6. Vehicle related service truck	1	1,155	1.3
7. Services provided to other city agencies		7,010	7.6
Sedans	3	4,130	
Wagons	2	2,880	
Total		$92,075	100.0

Table 7-4. Costs, by Division, 1972-1973

Division	Cost	% of Total Cost
Patrol	$4,463,325	58.5
Traffic	998,050	13.1
Detective	824,230	10.8
Special services	1,136,155	14.9
School crossing guards	208,240	2.7
Total	$7,630,000	100.0

veillance of its beat, and, except in special circumstances, not that of any other beat. The city of Bridgeport is divided into seventeen "beats" or areas in which patrol cars roam 24 hours a day. These beats are of varying sizes, depending on the density of the area and the incidence of crime there. Roughly speaking, the beats are laid out so that there are equal probabilities in all beats of receiving a citizen's call for service.

Patrol cars routinely patrol their beats until a call for service breaks this routine. When the central police station receives a call, the nearest police car (usually the one operating in the caller's beat) is dispatched to the scene. Other nearby cars are also alerted, and it is their responsibility to take over the routine patrol activity of the car responding to the call. Naturally, given these new duties, these cars cannot patrol their own beats as frequently. In particularly "rough" neighborhoods, the backup car must also go to the scene of the incident to be available to render assistance and to guard against vandalism on the patrol car actually responding to the call. Once the call for service is handled, both the responding patrol car and any backup car resume routine patrol activities.

Patrol division costs have been allocated to specific services according to the amount of police time spent on each type of service, under the assumption that the cost per unit time is the same for all services provided by the patrol division. This accounts for only a relatively small proportion of the patrol division's total cost, however, because patrols spend only 17 percent of their time responding to calls for service, the remaining time being free for routine patrol.

The cost of this routine patrol can be handled in two ways. Routine patrol could be treated as a separate type of service or as an indirect function that must be performed in order to be available to respond to calls for service. We have chosen the latter alternative and allocated the cost of routine patrol to the specific types of service in proportion to the time spent responding to calls for each type of service. This choice was made in part because police are allocated to beats in proportion to the number of calls for service. Thus, the greater the number of calls for service, the greater the routine patrol time.

The Bridgeport police department graciously provided data that enabled us to estimate the amount of time devoted to each type of service. Two types of data were made available: a large sample of incident reports, and a smaller sample of time reports.

Incident Reports.   Each call for service to which a patrol car responds must be written up in an incident report. These incident reports are then coded, processed, and summarized by the department's Records Division using the city's computer facilities. For this study, summary reports, giving the incident's code, the date, and the neighborhood[e] in which the incident occurred, were gathered for the months of January, April, and August, 1973. These incident reports provide a count of calls for police aid by type of service and location.

Time Reports.   Unfortunately, the monthly summary data show only the number of calls of each type, not the amount of time spent responding to each call. To determine how much time was spent responding to calls, it was necessary to use more detailed data, specifically individual incident reports coded for machine use. Because these reports include the time patrolmen went "out of service" to respond to a call and the time they returned to service, the time spent handling the call can be computed. The detailed reports for the first week of April 1973 have been used, providing a sample of 1,207 incidents.

Using the sample of time reports, it was possible to estimate the average time spent responding to each type of call. However, since this sample covers only one week, the number of calls for each type of service and the location of the calls might not be representative. For this reason the incident reports sample, covering a span of three months, was used to estimate the number of calls for each type of service by police grid (Fig. 7-2). By multiplying the time per incident times the number of incidents, the time spent responding to each type of call in each grid was estimated.[f] The cost of each type of ser-

[e] A neighborhood is defined to be one of 37 areas or grids, which the police department has devised for Bridgeport. See Figure 7-2, a map of the city with the grids numbered.

[f] A legitimate concern is that the time patrolmen spend on each call might vary from neighborhood to neighborhood, and that the application of a simple city-wide average time per incident might seriously misrepresent the actual allocation of police time in various neighborhoods. Fortunately, an examination of

vice was estimated simply by multiplying the cost per unit time by the time spent on each type of incident within each grid.

The services provided by the detective division are somewhat different from those of the patrol division. Most detective assignments follow up calls initially handled by the patrol division. The types of service rendered by the detective division are therefore constantly changing, depending on the nature of the calls for service and on their location throughout the city. Only certain calls receive any attention from the detective division. Incidents such as emergency medical treatment, family disputes, and nuisance receive no detective followup investigation. Major crimes, however, often require large inputs of detective time to gather evidence for trial, to track down a suspect, and so forth.

The costs of the detective division were allocated to specific services according to rough estimates provided by police officials of the detective time spent following up different types of cases. The relative magnitudes of these weightings are shown in Table 7-5. These weights, in combination with the incident reports from the patrol division, permitted the estimating of the detective time spent and thus the cost of each type of service in each grid.

In summary, patrol division expenses were allocated to types of service in proportion to the time spent on incidents of each type, and the detective division expenses were allocated in proportion to the time spent on followup of each type of service. Allocating the expenses of each of the other divisions to specific types of service was not possible. Fortunately, the mandates of the traffic and special duty services divisions are more narrowly defined than those of either the patrol or detective divisions.

Results

Table 7-6 displays our estimates of police expenditure by the type of service rendered. The work of the various special duty services and the traffic division (neither of which could be disaggregated into more specific services) accounts for about 15 and 13 percent, respectively, of all police expenditures. Another 38 percent of police resources is devoted to seven types of calls for service: motor vehicle thefts, 8 percent; alarms, 5 percent[g]; larceny, 5 percent; nuisances, 5

---

this question does not reveal that times per incident differ systematically across neighborhoods. The city of Bridgeport was divided into three groups of relatively homogenous neighborhoods, and, as Appendixes B and C show, the times per incident do not differ systematically across the three groups.

[g]The category "alarms" includes not only time spent responding to burglar and fire alarms but also time spent waiting for the owner to arrive to reset the alarm and secure the building.

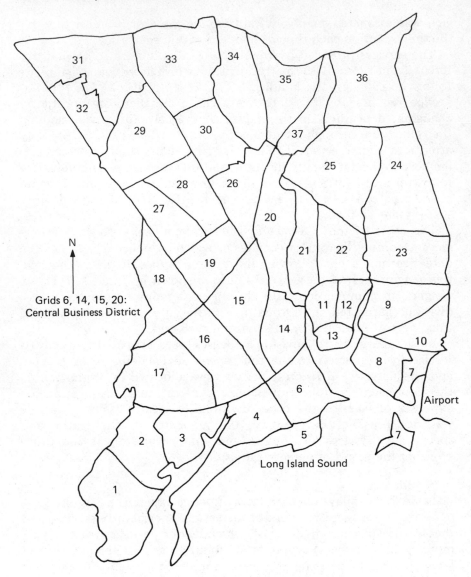

Grids 6, 14, 15, 20:
Central Business District

Long Island Sound

Airport

N

Figure 7-2. Crime Grids, Bridgeport, Connecticut

percent[h]; assaults, 5 percent; medical problems, 5 percent; and burglaries, 5 percent. The remaining third of police costs is devoted to a wide range of calls for service including disorderly conduct, vandalism, missing persons, abandoned autos, and lost and found property.

[h]"Nuisances" include barking dogs, other animal nuisances, fire crackers, littering offenses, and other minor nuisances.

Table 7–5. Degree of Detective Followup, by Type of Incident

| | Detective Followup Weightings | | |
| | *Light* | *Moderate* | *Substantial* |
Code and Incident	*(weighted 1)*	*(weighted 2)*	*(weighted 4)*
01 Homicide			x
02 Rape			x
03 Robbery			x
04 Assault			x
05 Burglary			x
06 Larceny < $50		x	
07 Larceny > $50			x
08 Auto Theft			x
09 Forgery			x
10 Other Larceny		x	
11 Weapons		x	
14 Sex Offenses			x
16 Narcotics			x
19 Kidnapping			x
20 Arson		x	
26 Property Damage	x		
38 Missing Person		x	
40 Suspicious Person	x		
43 Investigations		x	
44 Accidents		x	

Note: Other types of incidents do not require detective division follow-up or require only very limited action.

Source: Interviews with Bridgeport Police Department officials.

In summary, police services are not a single, homogeneous public good as some economists apparently assume. Quite the contrary, police departments provide a wide range of services that range along a continuum from pure public goods, which are jointly consumed over a large geographical area, to private goods, which are consumed by a single individual. It is important to recognize this heterogeniety of police services. Indeed, examination of the program budget shows that a few services account for a surprisingly high proportion of police costs. While one would expect assault, burglary, larceny, and vandalism to account for a relatively large part of the total police cost, one would not expect alarms and nuisances to account for so large a proportion of the cost of police services. While everyone knows the police spend some time enforcing traffic laws, motor vehicle theft, traffic division expenses, and other auto-related services account for a surprising 27 percent of police costs. In short, our results paint a rather different picture of the utilization of police resources than we had expected.

Table 7–6. Police Costs, by Type of Service, 1973

Type of Service	Estimated Annual Cost (Dollars)	% of Total
Special duty services division	$1,136,155	14.89
Traffic division	998,050	13.08
Motor vehicle theft	611,219	8.01
Burglar alarms	418,175	5.48
Nuisances (except abandoned auto)	403,795	5.29
Larceny (nonauto)	397,063	5.20
Assault	381,590	5.00
Medical assistance	368,591	4.83
Burglary	361,204	4.73
Damage to property	258,066	3.38
Disorderly conduct	224,568	2.94
School crossing guards	208,240	2.73
Family and children	178,234	2.34
Larceny (auto)	138,632	1.82
Motor vehicle violations	116,791	1.53
Accidents, auto	106,910	1.40
Drugs	105,814	1.39
Nuisances (abandoned auto)	104,758	1.37
Suspicion	99,806	1.31
Drunkeness	98,430	1.29
Missing person	87,898	1.15
Accidents, nonauto	71,301	0.93
Dead on arrival	65,775	0.86
Robbery	61,887	0.81
Internal functions	53,181	0.70
Property, Lost & Found	36,000	0.47
Justice violations	34,109	0.45
Vice	30,546	0.40
Process service	20,810	0.27
Arson	17,656	0.23
Weapons	17,523	0.23
Forgery	15,954	0.21
Sex offenses	15,625	0.20
Other larceny	15,530	0.20
Investigations	13,557	0.18
Found person	9,306	0.12
Escapes	7,461	0.10
Rape	3,909	0.05
Court violations	3,805	0.05
Homicide	2,103	0.03
Miscellaneous	329,714	4.32
	$7,629,741	100.00

Note: These services are defined in the Patrolman's Code Book for the Bridgeport Police Department.

PART II   FINANCING POLICE SERVICES
BY SPECIAL CHARGES

Although generally quick to endorse user charges for scarce resources, most economists would not favor such charges for police services for at least two reasons. First, they consider police services a pure public good that benefit large groups of residents jointly, so that charging for them would be inefficient. Second, they believe that the poor receive a disproportionate share of police services so that charging for them would be highly regressive.

The results of Part I, however, might lead one to question the first argument. Police services are not a single pure public good but a heterogeneous set of services including some private services. While it may be inappropriate to charge for all of the services, might it not be useful to charge for a subset of them? On the other hand, the argument that charges would be regressive is compelling, if it is correct. The data base used in Part I permits us to ask whether the police do in fact devote more resources to poor neighborhoods.

Part II is devoted to an examination of the efficiency of special charges and the distribution of police resources among income classes.

The Efficiency of Special Charges

It is useful to distinguish two types of special charges that might be imposed: user charges and class charges. Like a price in a market, a user charge is a charge for a specific service, which is withheld unless payment is made. For a charge to be a user charge, the individual must have a choice whether to consume the service and how much to consume. A class charge, on the other hand, is a charge made to a class of consumers who benefit from the service, unrelated to the specific level of consumption of individuals within that class. Under a class charge, an individual has the choice of entering a given class of consumers; once in the class, however, the individual must pay a fixed charge, which does not vary directly with the incremental cost of the quantities of services he consumes.[i] In the private sector, a membership fee in a private swimming club is an example of a class charge if the consumer pays to join the club but, having once joined, does not make additional payments for each swim.

Both types of charges provide an incentive to economize on re-

---

[i]We are grateful to Malcolm Getz for suggesting the distinction between user and class charges.

sources, but the user charge, because it is precisely related to particular consumer decisions and to the incremental cost of those decisions, provides the greater incentive. Under a class charge the individual confronts an incentive to economize only for those decisions that will change his classification. Nonetheless, depending on the definition of the classes, such charges could provide incentives that would improve economic efficiency.

The efficiency of class or user charges depends upon the sensitivity of demand to charges, the incremental cost of providing the service, the extent of spillovers to other consumers, and the administrative costs of imposing the charges. If demand is not responsive to charges, or if the marginal cost of the service is low, then the efficiency gains from charges will be small. When there are substantial positive spillovers from one class to another—as, for example, when enforcement in one area deters crime generally—charges will reduce efficiency because they will discourage the creation of this positive externality. Finally, the administrative cost of imposing the charges must be included in the efficiency calculation; indeed, they may be large enough to outweigh any gains in allocative efficiency.

In summary, charges vary along a continuum from general revenue financing, through class charges of increasing precision, to user charges. General revenue financing provides almost no incentive to reduce consumption of police services. Class charges provide such an incentive—an incentive that becomes stronger, the more precise the definition of the class. At the extreme level of precision, user charges provide the greatest incentive to economize on the use of scarce resources. For private goods, user charges are efficient. For pure public goods, a zero charge (e.g., general revenue financing) is efficient. For the intermediate case of goods with substantial externalities, class charges may be efficient depending on the nature of the spillover, the responsiveness of demand to charges, the marginal cost of the service, and the administrative cost of imposing charges. The efficient level of precision (i.e., the number of classes) depends on the relative magnitude of these factors.

Police Services.   Since the choice among different types of special charges depends upon the characteristics of the service, discussion of the efficiency of charges for police services should proceed service by service. To simplify this discussion, we have divided the many police services into the following five categories: private services, automobile services, services to city agencies, city-wide services, and neighborhood services.

Private Services.   A private service is one which is rendered to a specific individual or property with minimal spillovers to other individuals or properties. Examples include rendering medical assistance and guarding a building while waiting for an owner to reset the burglar alarm and secure the building.

Provided the demand for such services is responsive to price, charging individuals the marginal cost of the services they consume will increase economic efficiency. Since estimating the marginal cost of specific services is extremely difficult, however, any practical schedule of charges would undoubtedly be based on average cost. Police departments could rather easily estimate the average time spent on each type of service and the average cost per unit of police time in order to estimate the average cost of each service, much as we have done in the first part of this chapter.j

In addition to problems of estimating marginal cost, charges for private services present some practical administrative difficulties. While it would be relatively easy to identify the person who receives the services, and therefore to bill him, the administrative costs of doing so would not be trivial. Moreover, the rate of nonpayment is likely to be high both because of the poverty of some users of police services and because of citizen resistance to paying for previously "free" services which may be considered a right. In short, although it appears feasible to charge for some private services and modest efficiency gains are likely to exist, anticipated public resistance and high administrative costs may make user charges for private services impractical.

Automobile Services. Automobile services are those services provided to facilitate automobile transportation. The obvious examples include directing traffic, issuing traffic citations, recovering stolen autos, and so on. All traffic division services and many patrol division services relate specifically to automobiles.

Automobile users define a class of individuals who, if charged for operating an auto, might be expected to reduce the number of cars they own and shift to other forms of transportation, thereby increasing efficiency.k Since public transportation is often a fairly close substitute for automobiles especially for commuting, the choice of the

jIt might be argued that average cost estimated in this way approximates long run marginal cost. Since police services are extremely labor intensive, time devoted to the service is a reasonable basis for computing average cost. And, average cost per unit time can be assumed constant provided economies of scale are minimal. In short, although this form of average cost pricing would not be ideal, it probably approximates long run marginal cost pricing.

kIn addition, if the cost of auto services provided by police varies across municipalities, some readjustment of work place and residential locations could be expected.

auto mode of transportation is probably somewhat responsive to charges for public services.[1]

Perhaps the simplest way of charging auto users is a parking tax applied to all parking in the city. While metering of street parking and collection of taxes from private concerns with parking facilities would not be free, the number of concerns involved is relatively small so that enforcement and collection would be possible. An alternative is a license tag tax on all automobiles garaged in the city. Since suburban commuters would not pay the tag tax, and reverse commuters would not pay the parking tax, a combination of the two, with city residents exempted from paying the parking tax, might be preferable. In the absence of such charges, the beneficiaries would be either the auto users or owners of downtown properties (e.g., through higher values) or some combination; of course downtown assessments may already reflect any such values.

Services to City Agencies. Police services can be rendered to or for other agencies of city government. For example, in Bridgeport, school crossing guards serve the school system, another city department. Like residents, city agencies should be encouraged not to waste police resources. In most cases, it should be relatively easy to identify which services are provided to other agencies and to estimate at least their average cost. Charges could then be made against that agency's budget. Such charges might be expected to induce some economizing behavior by the agency itself, but the extent of economizing would depend upon the organization and the incentive structure within the agency. In addition, if the agency in turn charges consumers of its services, some behavior changes would probably be induced in residents as well. In both cases, modest efficiency gains might result with little added administrative cost.

City-wide Services. "City-wide services" are those services which, if provided to one person, are provided in some degree to all residents of the city. Technically, they are examples of pure public goods, but from the perspective of the city limits.[3] For example, police response to "offenses against the administration of justice" is consumed jointly by all residents. Since the cost of providing this type of service to an additional resident is zero, economic efficiency requires a zero price for the service. Consequently, financing city-wide services out of general revenue satisfies the requirement of economic efficiency.

[1]The same efficiency arguments obviously also apply to charges for the maintenance of streets in the city.

Neighborhood Services. By neighborhood service we mean any service which, when provided to one individual or property, substantially affects other individuals or properties in the same neighborhood, but which does not affect other neighborhoods in a significant way.[m] For example, control of disorderly conduct benefits a relatively limited geographic area. The class of people which benefits from these services includes primarily the residents of the neighborhood but also those who work, shop, or travel within it. A neighborhood charge is simply a class charge where the class is defined by residence in the neighborhood. The total cost of providing neighborhood services could be divided among the neighborhood's residents— according to property values, according to street frontage, or on a per capita basis.

A case for such neighborhood charges, based on economic efficiency, is implicit in Charles Tiebout's "A Pure Theory of Local Expenditures".[4] He argued that location choices can, under certain assumptions, reveal people's preferences for publicly provided goods and services and thus lead to efficiency in the provision of these goods and services. While Tiebout wrote of services produced by municipalities, his argument can be extended to neighborhood services financed by neighborhood charges. Neighborhood charges would provide an incentive to locate in neighborhoods where the cost of additional police protection equals the additional benefit the resident receives from it.

This incentive will not by itself lead to greater efficiency. "Supply"—the level and mix of police services provided—must also adjust in response to the movement of residents. In the Tiebout argument, a governmental unit corresponds to each geographic area over which charges vary. In the case of neighborhood charges, however, one city government would be responsible for deciding the level of service in many neighborhoods. For neighborhood charges to be efficient, city governments must have some mechanism for varying the level of service in response to the revealed preferences of residents.

Moreover, Tiebout's original argument is subject to criticism because of its restrictive assumptions, including among others: (1) the benefits from local public services do not spill over to other communities,[5] (2) within a jurisdiction public services are not subject to congestion,[6] (3) the choice of the community with the desired mix of public services does not affect other decisions (such as the choice

---

[m]"Neighborhood" is a necessarily ambiguous concept. One way to define a neighborhood would be by police beat, of which there are seventeen in Bridgeport. Under this definition, the average Bridgeport neighborhood contains about 9,000 people.

of housing or work place),[7] (4) people are perfectly mobile, and (5) the community fixes its mix of local services and acts to keep its size at the level that minimizes average costs. These assumptions are indeed heroic, but relaxing them seriously complicates the analysis. As the rapidly growing literature indicates, the Tiebout argument is subject to modification or questioning when these assumptions do not hold.

The point we wish to emphasize is simply that, if the Tiebout efficiency argument is correct in the abstract, then in practice the size of the geographical area for which charges should vary may be considerably smaller than present governmental units, especially for large central cities. Consequently, neighborhood charges are the logical extension of the Tiebout analysis.

The administrative problems of imposing neighborhood charges would be considerable. Again, the charge could be based on the average cost of providing neighborhood services to each neighborhood. These charges would have to be revised regularly, especially at the outset when the imposition of charges would presumably lead to changes in the level of services provided. In addition, neighborhoods must be defined so that the level of service is constant within them but spillovers between them are minimal. Because the boundaries would be arbitrary and the charges would be sensitive to their location, the choice of boundaries could become a troublesome political issue.[n]

In short, although the efficiency argument for neighborhood charges is simply the logical extension of the Tiebout argument, the administrative costs and practical difficulties of imposing neighborhood charges would be considerable. Moreover, the argument applies only to those services that do not spill over into adjacent neighborhoods; however, many police services do in fact spill over, invalidating the argument. The efficiency argument for neighborhood charges, while intuitively appealing in the context of Tiebout, is not necessarily persuasive for police services.

The Distributional Impact of Police Services

In this section we explore the distributional impact of police services by examining the incidence of police expenditures. Specifically, we ask, "Who receives police services and how much do they cost?"

[n]This boundary problem might be resolved by averaging charges across locations to create a smooth, continuous schedule of charges for the different areas of the city. This would eliminate wide differences in charges across neighborhood boundaries, but would complicate the administration of the charges considerably.

The motivations for doing so are two. First,the incidence of expenditures for government services is of interest in its own right, especially in the context of Seranno and other education equity cases. Second, to the extent that special charges are based on average cost, the incidence of expenditures is equivalent to the nominal incidence of special charges. Thus the calculations presented below are subject to a dual interpretation, as expenditure incidence or as service charge incidence. Readers who have no interest in special charges may nonetheless find the incidence calculations of some interest.[8]

Our procedure is quite simple. We begin by classifying all police services into the five categories discussed above. We then make estimates of who receives the services and how much they cost. For services received by city residents, we estimate the cost of services in each neighborhood. Finally, we estimate the relation between this cost and the income of the neighborhood. The calculations are admittedly crude,[o] but they provide some indication of the progressivity of expenditures relative to property taxes.

The classification of police services into the five categories discussed above is sometimes difficult. While the automobile services and services provided other city agencies are relatively easy to identify, few of the remaining services fit neatly into the major categories. There are both public and private aspects of many services, and spillovers from one neighborhood to another are often substantial. Despite the admitted ambiguity, we have classified the hundreds of different police services, ranging from "abandoned motor vehicle" to "responding to the wrong address," as private, auto, neighborhood, city-wide, or other-agency services. Since our classification is frankly subject to dispute, the details are presented together with the cost of each service in Appendix A to this chapter, so that the reader can perform sensitivity tests based on his own classification of services.

Table 7-7 presents the cost of police services by type of service based upon this classification. A surprisingly high percentage of the services subject to charges are accounted for by auto services; apparently automobile users are subsidized rather heavily by those who pay property taxes. The services categorized as private also comprise a surprisingly large percent of total police services. In short, with the exception of services provided to other city agencies, each type of

[o]The calculations concern the incidence of expenditures not the incidence of the benefits of reduced crime. In addition, all the calculations are nominal incidence estimates; they ignore any changes in prices or location which might be induced by charges. They also ignore any reductions in total cost caused by charging.

Table 7-7. Police Expenses, by Type of Service

Category[a]		Allocated Cost	% of Total
I.	Private	$1,240,450	16.3
II.	Auto	2,053,280	26.9
III.	Neighborhood Services	2,359,950	30.9
	A. Residential	1,616,880	68.5
	B. Commercial-Industrial	743,070	31.5
IV.	City-wide Services	1,768,110	23.2
V.	Services to Other City Agencies (School crossing guards)	208,240	2.7
	Total	$7,629,630	100.0

[a]For the specific services in each category and their cost, see Appendix A of this chapter.

service accounts for a substantial share of the total police budget. Thus the potential practical importance of special charges is not trivial.

Who receives these services? We have defined five groups, city residents, commercial and industrial property, city agencies, tax-exempt property, and suburban auto users, and tried to estimate the cost of the services each group receives. Because the services consumed by the last two groups cannot be identified from the police data, estimates had to be made based on other evidence.

To estimate the cost of auto services consumed by suburban drivers, we have used census data on commuting patterns and assumed that the cost of auto services is proportional to the number of trips ending in Bridgeport. Under this assumption, the proportion of auto services consumed by nonresidents was estimated to be 38 percent of the cost of auto services, or 10.3 percent of the total police budget.[P] A service charge on all Bridgeport parking would be distributed in the same way.

[P]The number of trips to Bridgeport by Bridgeport residents equals the number of work trips there (obtained from "Journey to Work," *1970 Census of Population*, PC (2)-60, Table 1) plus the number of non-work trips. The latter was estimated assuming that the ratio of trips for family business, civic, educational and recreational purposes to work trips in Bridgeport is the national average, 1.11 (obtained from U.S. Department of Transportation, Federal Highway Administration, *Nationwide Personal Transportation Study*, Report #10, p. 67) and that all such trips end in Bridgeport. The trips to Bridgeport from its suburbs were similarly estimated under the assumption that an arbitrary 20 percent of the non-work trips are to Bridgeport. Using these two admittedly crude estimates, the proportion of the cost of auto services received by nonresidents is simply the ratio of the trips from outside Bridgeport to the total number of trips there.

Table 7-8. Comparison of the Nominal Incidence of Expenditures and Property Taxes

Taxpayer Class	Property Tax	Percent of Total	Expenditures	Percent of Total
City commercial & industrial property[a]	$1,865,000	24.4	$1,001,000	13.1
City residents	5,765,000	75.6	5,084,000	66.6
Private services	—	—	1,240,000	
Auto services	—	—	1,271,000	
Neighborhood services	—	—	1,237,000	
Citywide services	—	—	1,336,000	
Other city agencies[b]	0	0	208,000	2.7
City tax-exempt properties	0	0	555,000	7.3
Suburban auto users	0	0	782,000	10.3
Total	$7,630,000	100.0	$7,630,000	100.0

[a]Where the data do not distinguish services provided to residential property from those provided to commercial or industrial property, the costs have been allocated to residential property. Consequently, the cost of services provided to commercial and industrial property are underestimated.

[b]The data only permitted the separate identification of the cost of school crossing guards. To the extent that other services are provided to city agencies, our estimate is biased downward.

To estimate the cost of neighborhood services consumed by tax-exempt institutions, we assumed (for lack of data) that they consume services in proportion to property values. Under this crude assumption, 23.5 percent of the cost of neighborhood services, or 7.3 percent of total police costs, go to tax-exempt properties.[9]

Table 7-8 summarizes these calculations. Suburban auto users and tax-exempt property receive services which account for roughly 17.6 percent of the total cost of police services. Another 2.7 percent goes to schools. Commercial and industrial property owners receive directly services which cost only 54 percent of their property tax payments while the corresponding figure for city residents is 88 percent.[q]

The Expenditures column of Table 7-8 can also be interpreted as an estimate of how much each group would pay under special charges. As the table indicates, special charges hold one distinct ad-

[q]These estimates undoubtedly overstate the special charges to residents and understate those for commercial and industrial properties because all the costs of private and city auto services have been allocated to residents. Moreover, commercial and industrial services included only those services that could be identified explicitly. Because of the calls for service codes used by the Bridgeport police, some commercial-industrial services are indistinguishable from residential services. In our calculations, these services are allocated to residential services, creating an upward bias.

vantage over the property tax: they reduce the tax burden of city residents and commercial and industrial property by extending the revenue base to automobile users who are not city residents and to presently tax-exempt institutions.[r] A total of 17 percent of the budget would be paid by these two groups.[s] In a time of rapidly rising city expenditures and concern about the high level of property taxes and their effect on location decisions, this extension may be quite attractive to city officials. Charges may be seen as a new source of revenue and an appealing way of shifting the tax burden to new groups.

Although in the aggregate the city taxpayers, including both residents and businesses, receive services that cost less than the property taxes they pay—and would be better off under special charges—substantial variations exist within each group. If the special charges are substantially more regressive than the property tax, then poor residents may be worse off under special charges even though the revenue base is extended to new groups.

Although the data have some limitations,[t] some indication of the nominal incidence of expenditures (and therefore special charges) relative to income and relative to the property taxes can be obtained. Using Census data and service cost data for each grid, we have estimated linear relationships between the expenditures for each type of service and median family income. For city-wide services, we assumed that expenditures are proportional to housing values; for other services, expenditures are estimated based on the amount of police time spent providing the service in each neighborhood. The relation between total expenditures and income was then obtained simply by summing the individual linear relations for the four types of service. The relation between property taxes and income was based on median house values obtained from the census.[u]

[r]Since people other than city residents consume some private services when they come to the city to work or shop, the cost of some private services might also be shifted to nonresidents. This extension of the tax base would probably be quite small, and in any event, we have no basis for estimating its magnitude.

[s]One important practical difficulty with charges is that they are not deductible from income as defined by the Internal Revenue Service. This means that the money cost of charges to city residents will increase if their increased income taxes are taken into account. Wherever ordinances can be drafted so that payments are treated as "taxes" rather than "charges" this problem is solved. In many cases, however, such a solution is extremely difficult legally.

[t]There are at least two important data limitations. The cost data can be allocated only as far as the police grid. Since individuals cannot be identified and since the census data used are tract averages, all individual variation in both the consumption of services and income are lost. In addition, the census data covers only residences and not commercial or industrial establishments.

[u]Property taxes were calculated so that total taxes predicted by the function equaled the total cost of police services. Formally, the equation estimated was:

The resulting tax and expenditure functions are reported in Table 7-9. The results are consistent with expectations. Property taxes (and, therefore, expenditures for city-wide services) are nearly proportional to income, but expenditures for auto services increase more than proportionately with income. Both results are statistically significant. Although the relation between the cost of private and neighborhood services and income is not statistically significant, the direction of the relation is as anticipated—as income increases, the use of these services declines absolutely. Total expenditures for all types of services apparently also decline absolutely with income. A 1 percent increase in income is associated with a 0.3 percent drop in total expenditures.

Figure 7-3 graphs the estimated incidence functions for total expenditures and property taxes. Because of the services suburban auto users and tax-exempt property consumed, total expenditures at the 1970 median Bridgeport income of $9,800 lies below that of the property tax payment allocable to police services ($128 and $145, respectively).

Interpreted as expenditure functions, these results suggest that the incidence of police services is progressive in a limited sense: more police resources per family are devoted to poor neighborhoods than to rich ones. This result is hardly surprising since police are deployed on the basis of calls for service. Moreover, while the incidence of expenditures is progressive, the incidence of crime itself is undoubtedly regressive. Whether the *reduction* in crime rates resulting from enforcement efforts is distributed regressively or progressively is an important unanswered question.

An alternative way of interpreting the results in Table 7-9 is as special charge regressions. Viewed this way, they show that special charges, except for auto service charges, would be highly regressive relative to both income and property taxes. Indeed, as Figure 7-3

---

where

$$B_i = b_o + b\, Y_i$$

B_i : Base for the tax (property value)

Y_i : Income

The desired function is

$$T_i = t\, B_i = t\, b_o + tb\, Y_i$$

The tax rate, t, was chosen to satisfy the constraint that taxes sum to the total cost, T:

$$T = \Sigma\, T_i = n\, t\, (b_o + bY)$$ where n is the number of families.

Table 7-9. Nominal Incidence Regressions for Property Taxes and Police Expenditures for City Residents

Dependent Variable	Coefficients		R^2	Estimated Income Elasticity
	Intercept ($)	Median Family Income ($000)		
Residential property taxes per family[b]	3.24	14.4 (6.76)[a]	0.57	0.978
Private service expenditures per family[c]	86.83	–5.65 (1.45)	0.06	–1.787
Neighborhood service expenditures per family[d]	89.65	–5.95 (1.83)	0.09	–1.886
Auto service expenditures per family[e]	–10.17	4.27 (6.74)	0.56	1.318
Citywide service per family[f]	0.75	3.33 (6.76)	0.57	0.978
Total expenditures per family[g]	167.06	–4.00	—	–0.308

Note: These regressions were estimated using 37 observations, one for each of the 37 police grids in Bridgeport.

The median family income, the number of families per grid, house value per grid, and median auto ownership per grid were derived from census tract data. Since the grid boundaries differ from the census tract boundaries, grid data were estimated based on the fraction of land area in each tract. Each regression was of the form: dependent variable = $a + b$ * median family income.

[a]T-statistics are in parentheses.

[b]Property taxes per family = 0.0538 * median house value. The effective property tax rate for residential property in Bridgeport in 1970 was 5.38%. (See text footnote u for detailed explanation.)

[c]Private service expenditures per family = total private expenditures for the grid divided by the number of families in the grid.

[d]Neighborhood service expenditure per family = 0.765 * total neighborhood service expenditures divided by the number of families per grid. For Bridgeport, 76.5% of the property is currently taxable, the rest being tax exempt.

[e]Auto service expenditures per family = 9.15 * (1.09 + (5.478 * median auto ownership)). Expenditure per family is equal to total expenditure per trip times the trips per family. The total annualized expenditure per average daily trip is $9.15. The average trips per day per family is estimated from auto ownership per family by 1.09 + (5.478 * auto ownership), derived from Appendix C of Walter Oi and Paul Shudiner, *An Analysis of Urban Transportation Demands* (Northwestern University Press, Evanston, Ill., 1962).

[f]This regression is the same as the property tax regression.

[g]The total expenditures coefficients are simply the sum of the private, auto, neighborhood and city-wide coefficients; the equation was not estimated separately. (Formally, $E = \sum_i E_i = \sum_i (a_i + b_i Y) = \sum_i a_i + (\sum b_i) Y$.)

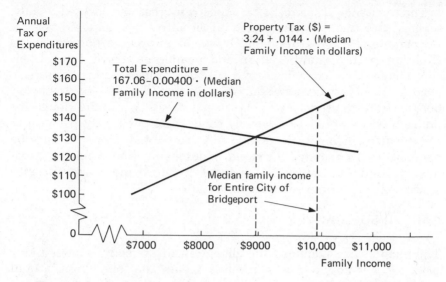

Figure 7-3. Nominal Incidence of Property Tax and Total Expenditures

sharply illustrates, total charges decline absolutely with increases in income.[v]

Assessment of Special Charges

Based on this evidence on the incidence of special charges and our discussion of their efficiency, we conclude that the conventional wisdom on user charges is largely correct. While user charges for private services would be efficient, they appear to be highly regressive and difficult to administer. Because of spillovers among neighborhoods, charging for neighborhood services would be inefficient as well as regressive. While it would be desirable in principle to charge other city agencies for police services, the bureaucratic resistance to doing so would be high, and moreover, it is not clear that organizational incentives would produce the desired response to the charges. Together with city-wide services,[w] these services for which charges appear inappropriate constitute 73 percent of total police costs.

[v]We should point out that while magnitudes would change, these conclusions would probably not change under alternative classifications of services. If free patrol time (time spent patrolling) were considered a neighborhood service (instead of being allocated to other services as we have done), the charges would be even more regressive. On the other hand if more services were classified as city wide instead of neighborhood services, then charges would appear less regressive.

[w]Although for efficiency, city-wide services should be financed through general revenues, such general revenues might be appropriately collected from traditionally tax-exempt institutions, either to raise revenue or for equity reasons.

The remaining 27 percent of police resources are devoted to auto services. For them, a class charge on all auto users, imposed as a tax on parking,[x] may be desirable. It would improve efficiency in the choice of mode of transportation; and it would be progressive—a 1 percent increase in income leads to a 1.3 percent increase in auto service charges. It is horizontally equitable, in that the class of users who benefit from the service would also pay for it. While the charge for police services would be relatively small ($32 per family per year at the median income), it could—and we would argue should—be combined with a charge for street maintenance that would approximately double the auto class charge.[y] In short, the charge for auto services merits further serious consideration.

PART III SUMMARY

This chapter has examined the allocation of police resources, asking what services cost and who receives them. The following is a brief summary of the findings.

The police budget understates the social cost of police services by about 19 percent because labor's fringe benefits appear elsewhere in the budget and because interest and depreciation for capital goods simply do not appear in the current fund budget.

The police provide not a single service but a wide range of services ranging from private goods to pure public goods. Moreover, the proportion of resources devoted to some services is somewhat surprising. Services related to the automobile consume 27 percent of the total police resource; 8 percent are devoted to motor vehicle theft alone. Nuisances, alarms, and medical assistance, none of which is a crime prevention activity, each accounts for 5 percent of total cost.

The incidence of expenditures is much as expected. More resources per family are devoted to poor neighborhoods than to rich ones, not only relatively but absolutely. An exception is auto services. As income increases, the cost of auto services received increased more than proportionately. Moreover, an estimated 38 percent of auto services go to suburban auto users who commute to the city.

In addition to the empirical study of the allocation of police resources, this chapter has examined the possibility of financing police

[x]This might be combined with a tag tax on all vehicles housed in the city which would then be exempted from the parking tax.

[y]Direct costs (without adjustments for fringe benefits or capital expenses) for street lighting, road maintenance, pavement replacement, snow and ice removal, street signs, offstreet parking, and street sweeping amount to almost $1.7 million compared to $2 million of direct plus imputed costs of police auto services.

services through special charges imposed on those who receive them. With two exceptions we have found them inadvisable because of spillovers, which render them inefficient; high administrative costs, which render them impractical; and regressivity, which renders them unfair.

One exception is a charge to tax-exempt institutions that benefit from police services. If legal problems of imposing such a charge could be solved, it would raise additional revenue. Moreover, some might consider such a charge more equitable.

The other exception might be a class charge imposed on auto users through a parking tax to cover the cost of police and street maintenance services they receive. Such a charge should be more efficient than property tax financing. Moreover, by eliminating an implicit subsidy of auto users by nonauto users, it would be horizontally equitable.

✳ *Appendix 7–A*

Table 7A-1. Private Allocation of Patrol and Detective Division Costs

Type of Service	% of Patrol	$(Patrol)	% of Detective	$(Detective)	Total $	% of Total Allocation
Larceny–nonauto–minor ($50) (bike, credit card, animal theft, pickpocket)	6.3	72,835	12.4	10,459	83,294	6.7
Larceny–nonauto–major ($50) (bike, credit card, animal theft, pickpocket)	6.1	70,522	49.7	41,922	112,444	9.1
Missing person	4.4	50,869	16.5	13,918	64,787	5.2
Found person	.7	8,093			8,093	.6
Suspicion	5.3	61,274	13.5	11,387	72,661	5.9
Alarms	33.6	388,451			388,451	31.3
Property	1.5	17,342			17,342	1.4
Accidents, nonauto	4.6	53,181	7.8	6,579	59,760	4.8
Medical problems	31.2	360,705			360,705	29.0
Process service	1.8	20,810			20,810	1.7
Internal functions	4.6	53,181			53,181	4.3
		1,157,263		84,265	1,241,528	

Table 7A-2. Auto Allocation of Patrol and Detective Division Costs

Type of Service	% of Patrol	$(Patrol)	% of Detective	$(Detective)	Total $	% of Total Allocation
Larceny-auto-minor	6.0	45,690	2.1	6,253	51,943	4.9
Larceny-auto-major	7.2	54,828	10.7	31,861	86,689	8.2
Motor vehicle theft	45.0	340,719	83.2	247,739	588,458	55.8
Nuisances (abandoned vehicle)	13.8	104,758	—	—	104,758	9.9
Accidents, auto	12.6	95,297	3.9	11,613	106,910	10.1
Motor vehicle violations	15.3	116,184	—	—	116,184	11.0
		757,476		297,466	1,054,942	

Note: In addition there is an allocation of $998,053 for traffic services.

Table 7A–3. City-wide Allocation of Patrol and Detective Division Costs

Type of Service	% of Patrol	$ (Patrol)	% of Detective	$ (Detective)	Total $	% of Total Allocation
Assault	0.4	2,132	1.3	843	2,975	0.5
Burglary (with violence)	8.4	47,966	28.5	18,491	66,457	10.5
Larceny–nonauto–minor ($50) (mail, of firearms, checks)	4.3	24,516	4.6	2,985	27,501	4.3
Larceny–nonauto–major ($50) (mail, of firearms, checks)	3.6	20,252	16.3	10,576	30,828	4.9
Forgery	0.9	5,330	2.0	1,298	6,628	1.0
Other larceny offenses (embezzlement, extortion, etc.)	2.6	14,923	—	—	14,923	2.4
Commercialized Vice	4.1	23,450	8.8	5,710	29,160	4.6
Sex offenses	0.9	5,330	1.4	908	6,238	1.0
Drugs	12.6	71,416	35.3	22,903	94,319	14.9
Court Violations	0.6	3,198	—	—	3,198	0.5
Offenses against adm. of justice	6.0	34,109	—	—	34,109	5.4
Escapes	1.3	7,461	—	—	7,461	1.2
Dead on Arrival	11.3	63,955	—	—	63,955	10.1
Property	0.2	1,066	—	—	1,066	0.2
Investigation	1.3	7,461	1.8	1,168	8,629	1.4
Miscellaneous	41.5	235,567	—	—	235,567	37.2
		568,132		64,882	633,014	

Note: In addition there is an allocation of $1,136,159 for Special Duty Service.

Table 7A-4. Residential Allocation of Patrol and Detective Division Costs

Type of Service	% of Patrol	$(Patrol)	% of Detective	$(Detective)	Total $	% of Total Allocation
Homicide	0.1	982	.1	241	1,223	0.1
Rape	0.2	2,946	.4	963	3,909	0.2
Robbery	1.9	26,514	6.9	16,615	43,129	2.7
Assault	16.1	221,930	49.3	118,715	340,645	21.1
Burglary	5.3	12,667	13.2	31,786	104,453	6.5
Larceny from residence	0.1	982	.1	241	1,223	0.1
Weapons	0.9	12,766	1.4	3,371	16,137	1.0
Drunkeness	7.1	97,217	—	—	97,217	6.0
Arson	0.8	10,802	.8	1,926	12,728	0.8
Disorderly conduct	12.1	166,939	—	—	166,939	10.3
Family & children	11.1	153,191	10.4	25,043	178,234	11.0
Damage to property	15.6	214,074	17.4	41,899	255,973	15.5
Nuisances (other than abandoned auto)	28.7	394,089	—	—	394,089	24.4
		1,375,099		240,800	1,615,899	

Table 7A-5.   Commercial-Industrial Allocation of Patrol and Detective Division Costs

Type of Service	% of Patrol	$(Patrol)	% of Detective
Homicide	.1	607	.2
Robbery	1.9	11,526	5.3
Assault	4.1	24,871	9.6
Burglary	21.9	132,850	42.1
Larceny–nonauto–minor	12.8	77,647	7.8
Larceny–nonauto–major	5.6	33,971	14.3
Motor vehicle theft	2.2	13,346	6.9
Forgery	1.2	7,279	1.5
Other larceny offenses	.1	607	—
Weapons	.2	1,213	.2
Commercialized vice	.2	1,213	.2
Sex offenses	1.3	7,886	1.1
Drugs	1.4	8,493	2.2
Drunkeness	.2	1,213	—
Arson	.7	4,246	.5
Disorderly conduct	9.5	57,629	—
Damage to property	.3	1,820	.2
Court violations	.1	607	—
Nuisances	1.6	9,706	—
Dead on arrival	.3	1,820	—
Missing person	3.0	18,199	3.6
Found person	.2	1,213	—
Suspicion	3.8	23,052	3.0
Alarms	4.9	29,724	—
Property	2.9	17,592	—
Investigations	.7	4,246	.5
Accidents	1.7	10,313	.9
Motor vehicle violations	.1	607	—
Medical problems	1.3	7,886	—
No incident known	.02	121	—
Miscellaneous	15.5	94,026	—
		605,529	

$(Detective)	Total $	% of Total Allocation
273	880	.1
7,232	18,758	2.5
13,099	37,970	5.1
57,444	190,294	25.6
10,643	88,290	11.9
19,512	53,483	7.2
9,415	22,761	3.1
2,047	9,326	1.3
—	607	.1
273	1,386	.2
273	1,386	.2
1,501	9,387	1.3
3,002	11,495	1.5
—	1,213	.2
682	4,928	.7
—	57,629	7.8
273	2,093	.3
—	607	.1
—	9,706	1.3
—	1,820	.2
4,912	23,111	3.1
—	1,213	.2
4,093	27,145	3.6
—	29,724	4.0
—	17,592	2.4
682	4,928	.7
1,228	11,541	1.6
—	607	.1
—	7,886	1.1
—	121	.02
—	94,026	12.7
136,584	742,113	

❋ *Appendix 7–B*

Table 7B-1. Mean Times per Incident for High Incidence Calls for Service, by Section of the City

Code and Call for Service	City-wide Mean (Minutes)	Section I	Section II	Section III
		(Entries give mean times and, in parentheses, the number of incidents used to compute the mean times)		
409 Simple assault	24.9	24.0 (9)	27.2 (13)	18.0 (2)
801 Auto theft	18.6	21.7 (24)	15.3 (20)	17.4 (8)
802 Recovered auto	33.1	35.1 (29)	25.8 (12)	40.5 (4)
2405 Family dispute	22.5	20.1 (22)	24.1 (17)	27.6 (5)
2602 Criminal mischief	20.3	22.2 (6)	21.1 (15)	16.3 (4)
2604 Window breaking	16.8	18.5 (11)	16.6 (9)	15.9 (7)
2408 Abandoned motor vehicle	16.3	22.8 (10)	14.5 (14)	12.7 (9)
4101 Burglar alarm	19.6	20.5 (21)	18.5 (21)	20.5 (4)
4505 M.V.–evading responsibility	37.8	36.6 (17)	40.1 (9)	—
4602 Medical assistance rendered	25.2	24.4 (49)	27.5 (15)	26.0 (7)
4901 Incident in "unfound"	11.5	11.2 (22)	13.0 (10)	10.0 (3)

Note: Section I can be generally characterized as central, poor, and predominantly black. It includes grids 3, 4, 6, 9, 11, 12, 13, 14, 15, 34. Section II is less central, less poor, and less black. It includes grids, 1, 2, 5, 7, 8, 10, 16, 17, 20, 21, 22, 23, 30, 33. Section III is middle class and includes grids 18, 19, 24, 25, 26, 27, 28, 29, 31, 32, 35, 36, 37.

※ *Appendix 7–C*

Table 7C-1. Mean Times per Incident, by General Category of Call, for Broadly Defined Sections of City

Category	City-wide Mean Time (Minutes)	Section I	Section II	Section III
1. Thefts of all kinds	27.52	30.90	22.80	31.20
2. Assaults of all kinds	29.38	33.00	27.20	25.00
3. Vice	30.00	30.00	—	—
4. Breach of the peace	25.86	25.60	25.78	27.83
5. Family disputes	22.50	20.09	24.06	27.60
6. Property damage	20.53	22.00	21.80	14.08
7. Court violations	58.50	63.33	—	44.00
8. Nuisances	20.08	23.40	18.90	16.77
9. Missing people or property	27.39	23.20	27.60	32.25
10. Alarms	19.64	21.85	17.81	18.13
11. Accidents	26.76	28.60	27.32	17.71
12. Medical problems	40.00	32.51	46.00	62.30
13. No incident	12.00	11.00	13.00	10.00
14. Miscellaneous	19.00	18.50	17.50	22.90

Note: Section I can be generally characterized as central, poor, and predominantly black. It includes grids 3, 4, 6, 9, 11, 12, 13, 14, 15, 34. Section II is less central, less poor, and less black. It includes grids, 1, 2, 5, 7, 8, 10, 16, 17, 20, 21, 22, 23, 30, 33. Section III is middle class and includes grids 18, 19, 24, 25, 26, 27, 28, 29, 31, 32, 35, 36, 37.

One of the more controversial types of special charge is the charge for neighborhood services. As mentioned in the previous sections, roughly one-third of the total police budget is devoted to providing neighborhood services as we have defined them. The large magnitude of this number does not necessarily imply that charges for such services merit further investigation. If the spatial variation in the cost of neighborhood services were small, then other, simpler taxes (such as a property or head tax) will differ very little from a neighborhood charge and will avoid all its administrative complexities. For this reason it is important to examine the spatial variation in the cost of neighborhood services.

Table 7D–1 points up what is commonly known: the number of incidents that require police patrol and detective time varies substantially from one area of a city to another. The patrol and detective costs attributable to grids (zones as defined by the Bridgeport police department) vary from $6,960 per year for a grid in the northern section of the city to $155,340 for a heavily populated central grid. Put on a per square mile and on a per capita basis, disparities are even more pronounced: $23,590 per square mile for grid 7, a sparsely populated coastal area, to $448,830 per square mile in a densely settled central grid; and $5.18 per capita for grid 7 to $316.58 per capita for grid 14 in the heart of the central business district. Typical grids incur costs for neighborhood services of between $80,000 and $250,000 per square mile and of between $10 and $30 per capita per year. Other than the high values attributable to the most

Table 7D-1.   Spatial Variation in Annual Neighborhood Service Costs

Grid	Section of City [a]	Neighborhood Costs	Percent of Total	Costs per Square Mile	Costs per Person
1	II	$ 62,620	2.66	$ 94,880	$ 17.12
2	II	68,200	2.90	162,380	18.29
3	I	91,090	3.87	189,770	35.12
4	I	62,260	2.65	151,850	17.86
5	II	34,020	1.45	109,740	22.29
6	I	93,370	3.97	194,520	21.74
7	II	8,020	0.34	23,590	5.18
8	II	49,390	2.10	137,190	27.35
9	I	51,300	2.18	131,540	14.66
10	II	43,630	1.85	128,320	24.16
11	I	46,470	1.97	331,930	20.22
12	I	54,540	2.32	389,570	13.13
13	I	53,860	2.29	448,830	52.44
14	I	142,640	6.06	324,180	133.30
15	I	140,690	5.98	234,480	14.97
16	II	155,340	6.60	231,850	17.85
17	II	80,030	3.40	109,630	16.84
18	III	40,150	1.71	81,940	8.59
19	III	59,160	2.51	147,900	13.20
20	II	42,670	1.81	79,020	29.39
21	II	71,000	3.02	244,830	11.70
22	II	89,050	3.78	228,330	15.74
23	II	62,040	2.64	110,790	10.04
24	III	60,410	2.57	85,080	8.64
25	III	96,860	4.12	98,840	24.76
26	III	44,570	1.89	92,850	12.18
27	III	42,900	1.82	84,120	11.39
28	III	50,600	2.15	95,470	9.65
29	III	36,910	1.57	53,490	8.81
30	II	35,250	1.50	95,270	16.58
31	III	43,210	1.84	60,010	15.63
32	III	12,610	0.54	39,410	7.43
33	II	103,170	4.38	112,140	41.00
34	I	116,250	4.94	152,960	16.22
35	III	46,750	1.99	93,500	26.38
36	III	55,500	2.36	67,680	24.63
37	III	6,960	0.30	27,840	11.74
Total		$2,353,490	100.00		

[a]The City of Bridgeport has been divided into three reasonably homogeneous sections. Section I can be generally characterized as central, poor, and predominantly black. Section II is less central, less poor, and less black. Section III is solidly middle class. Consult the grid map of Bridgeport included in this chapter.

central parts and the somewhat smaller values found for several of the city's "fringe" grids there is little that is systematic about the location of the per square mile or per capita costs of patrol and detective services.

✻   *Chapter 8*

Findings and Implications

John R. Meyer
John M. Quigley

Small cities, at least in the northeastern part of the United States, face many of the same financial problems as their larger brethren. They are caught in the same squeeze between ever-increasing demands for various kinds of public services and a less-than-proportionate increase in the property tax base so commonly relied on to finance these services. There are two obvious escapes from this squeeze. One is for local government to find new sources of revenue; the other is to reduce outlays.

Several different options can be identified, of course, for achieving these goals of increasing revenues or reducing costs. Indeed, as noted in the introductory chapter, the research reported in this volume was largely motivated by the presumption that at least some of the adverse financial consequences of postwar urban development could be alleviated by finding new revenues for central cities. Part II of this volume specifically addresses these issues, analyzing several policies often proposed as means of expanding revenues available to cities. Three alternatives are explored in particular detail: (1) policies to stimulate the economic growth of the central city, often described as "bringing industry back," or more generally as "redevelopment" policies; (2) policies designed to expand the revenue base by altering the tax-exempt status of private institutions; and (3) policies designed to increase the tax base directly by supplementing or replacing current property taxes with local income or payroll taxes.

The "redevelopment" option is explored in depth in Chapter Two. There, Malcolm Getz and Robert Leone discuss the efficacy and merit of a number of programs designed to attract industry to central city locations. In contrast to many discussions of the "redevelopment issue," their policy arguments are based upon a factual analysis of the recent history of industrial location and relocation decisions within the New Haven metropolitan area. In general, they found that many major efforts to attract large scale manufacturing industry to particular areas have been ill founded, but that a number of more modest and particularized redevelopment policies may be somewhat effective.

Their discussion of local development policies also highlights the inherent difficulty in drawing unqualified inferences from limited data. In their New Haven analysis, they clearly document the trend toward suburban or otherwise peripheral location of manufacturing establishments, trends that have also been observed in many of the country's larger metropolitan areas. They also found—echoing the findings of many studies for other cities—that a large proportion of new firms are "born" within the central city, in manufacturing as well as other sectors of the economy. Since new firms tend to be relatively small, this evidence of comparative advantage of the central city as an incubator could have important policy implications. For example, it suggests that the local public sector might well emphasize the "brokering of information" as a development policy. To illustrate: the maintenance of an up-to-date inventory of available commercial space might provide, at little cost, potential new firms with otherwise expensive information about sites, rents, and locational characteristics. The local public sector might also usefully act as an intermediary in providing systematic information about potential new firms to credit or other financial institutions, since proper financing can have a particularly important effect upon the viability of new, small firms.

These policies are hardly dramatic, especially when compared to ambitious programs of publicly supported physical renewal. Nevertheless, if the experiences of New Haven and many other metropolitan areas are at all typical, many of the reasons why larger manufacturing enterprises are increasingly attracted to the suburbs—or otherwise away from older central cities—are firmly rooted in very basic considerations of economic efficiency. If so, it may be very unwise policy to attempt to alter these location patterns, that is, to move against these basic and deeply rooted trends.

A massive effort by government to alter these location decisions would apparently be justified only if one could identify very substantial social costs that are omitted from the private calculus that now promotes employment decentralization. Such social costs, if they exist, could be "transition costs" associated with abandonment of social overhead capital and other investments in the central city. The very fact, however, that most physical renewal involves a demolition of such capital argues against any finding that great values are embedded in such investments. Another potential social cost of employment decentralization could be the "abandonment" of minorities locked into central city residential locations; if true, the question then is whether policies aimed at achieving housing desegregation or greater mobility for the urban poor might not be more appropriate than physical renewal policies.

Of course, policies that would modify existing tax burdens in central cities could also significantly affect the location patterns of industry and households. For example, to the extent that a payroll or income tax were substituted for a property tax or the property tax incidence were lightened by eliminating exemptions, taxpaying industry and households might find moving to or staying in the central city at least marginally more attractive than otherwise. Of course, revisions of local tax policy might also work in unexpected or perverse ways. For example, if a payroll or an income tax were substituted for the property tax, taxpaying industry or households might find location in the central city marginally more attractive than otherwise. However, firms using relatively more labor and less capital might have more incentive to relocate outside central city boundaries. In addition, if the institutions that are now exempt from property taxes perform functions that would otherwise be provided by government, the *net* fiscal impact of eliminating property tax exemptions might result in larger tax burdens for central city property owners. Evidence relevant to evaluating these various possibilities, in the particular context of New Haven, is the concern of Chapters Three and Four.

In Chapter Three, Robert Leone and John Meyer focus on the tax exemption question. They analyzed in some detail the impact of New Haven's largest tax-exempt institution, Yale University, upon the city. The analysis attempts to quantify the costs imposed on the city by the presence of the University and the services provided by the University, in turn, to local residents. By considering both revenues and services, both costs and benefits, this case study permits evaluation of the net impact of the tax-exempt institution upon the central city and upon the larger community. Measured on the basis of the costs of the services provided, Yale apparently provides more in terms of benefits than it receives in city services.

Overall, the analysis suggests that the net impact of taxes foregone and services provided is not large. However, the results also indicate that only about 35 percent of the services provided by Yale are consumed by residents of the city of New Haven. In this particular case, therefore, the central city provides a significant implicit subsidy to residents in the suburbs and to others throughout the state of Connecticut, since the costs of the implicit subsidy (as imposed by state law) are now borne by residents of the central city in the form of higher property taxes. The estimates thus suggest that if tax exemption is justified for Yale or similar institutions, the subsidy should be provided in large part by higher levels of government. In the Connecticut context, metropolitan or state populations apparently should bear some of the costs of Yale's tax exemption.

The case study of tax exemption nevertheless ends with somewhat ambiguous implications for public policy. Specifically, to interpret the evidence better, more information is needed on the demand for public services, those provided by the public sector and by particular tax-exempt institutions. For example, of the $1.6 million in public services provided by Yale to local residents, three-quarters is attributable to the costs of operating the University art gallery and the natural history museum. One may legitimately question whether the willingness-to-pay criterion would reveal that New Havenites, or Connecticut residents in general, place such a high value on these services. On the other hand, a very substantial portion of the city's costs incurred to serve Yale (approximately two-thirds of a total of $1.2 million) are for fire protection, protection that apparently is quite expensive and well beyond what the University might sensibly buy for itself.

In Chapter Four, Christopher Gadsden and Roger Schmenner explore in considerable depth local income taxation as an alternative to the taxation of real property. Their legal and economic analysis treats the history of local income taxation and evaluates the advantages and the problems associated with alternative forms of local income taxation. They conclude that the taxation of locally generated income is preferable on a number of grounds to the taxation of real property, and they present a crude quantitative analysis of the possible short-run effect of income taxation upon the city of New Haven.

For New Haven, it appears that a payroll or income tax substituted for the property tax would improve the fiscal position of the central city. Specifically, the size of the tax-exempt sector in New Haven is such that a nontrivial portion of any new payroll or income tax would be imposed upon professional workers in institutions that are currently paying no local property taxes. For a variety of reasons, it seems highly unlikely that many of these tax-exempt institutions would adjust to the imposition of a payroll or income tax on their employees by removing themselves from New

Haven. For example, Yale, like most universities and many property tax-exempt institutions, is very heavily invested in real estate. (Some might even argue overinvested, in part, because their real estate is tax exempt.) Moreover, tradition and other sentiments may lead to a strong attachment between certain nonprofit institutions and the central cities in which they are located.

Of course, much also depends on who ultimately bears any new taxes that might be imposed upon tax-exempt institutions. It is at least theoretically possible that new income or payroll taxes could be borne by (1) the institutions themselves; or (2) their employees; or (3) passed on to the consumers of their services—e.g., in the form of higher tuitions or tithes or bed charges. Little good evidence is now available to resolve this question of incidence; however to the extent the institutions themselves can escape incidence (that is, transfer it to their employees or to their consumers or other constituencies) there will be little incentive for relocation. In addition, one important class of tax-exempt properties in most central cities— governments themselves (such as federal and state institutions and establishments)—may be particularly insensitive to property tax considerations when making location decisions. Agencies of government are particularly well equipped to place the cost of any new payroll or income tax on their constituencies, and they are often "locked in" to central city sites for noneconomic reasons.

In the same vein, many nonexempt institutions that commonly remain within central cities often are in a particularly advantageous position to pass along cost increases (e.g., public utilities and financial institutions).

A case can also be made for substituting an income or payroll tax for the property tax on equity grounds. Indeed, such a case is argued in Chapter Four. It should be clear, though, that the equity issue is quite independent of the location-impact problem.

In Part III, the "other" solution to alleviating the demand-cost squeeze—reducing costs—is explored. Specifically, an investigation was made of how certain selected public services might be provided more efficiently or with a lower budget. In Chapter Five, Peter Kemper and John Quigley investigate municipal refuse collection; in Chapter Six, Malcolm Getz and Robert Leone analyze the provision of fire protection and firefighting services; and in Chapter Seven, Peter Kemper and Roger Schmenner investigate the provision of police services.

These three analyses share a common conceptual and empirical focus. For each, an attempt was made to define and measure service output and to investigate the distribution of services and of costs among populations, neighborhoods, and land use types. Each of these chapters also addresses the difficult question of pricing policy. An effort was made to analyze how alternative pricing mechanisms could be introduced to improve efficiency in service delivery and to expand the revenue base of the central city. Several findings are common to all these analyses and suggestive of policies that might provide stronger incentives for economic efficiency in the allocation of resources and increased productive efficiency in the public sector.

For refuse, strong arguments can be made for the imposition of specific collection charges, at least for charges that vary with the frequency and the location of the pickup. The Connecticut evidence also suggests that franchised or contract collection might provide a cheaper alternative to municipal provision by a city agency. The only apparent arguments against relying more on the private sector for refuse collection would appear to be easily met. For example, as long as bidding is truly competitive, economies of density could be preserved by allowing private contractors to bid for collection franchises or contracts along particular city routes. Similarly, periodic renewal (e.g., annually) or reasonably tight contract specification and enforcement could ward off shortfalls of service—perhaps at least as easily as when done by a civil service bureaucracy.

For fire protection, the evidence is less clear that more involvement of the private sector is desirable. The analysis indicates, however, that as long as the risks of conflagration are not "too great," it would be possible to finance fire services out of particular charges reflecting the probability of fire loss to specific properties. Moreover, the mechanism for establishing and calibrating such specific charges already exists, in the form of insurance premiums paid in the private market. For example, one relatively simple way to assess "probabilistic" charges for fire protection would be as a surcharge or percentage of insurance premiums (either as paid or payable if underwritten). One could also imagine more complex pricing schemes in which the charges for protection were varied to encourage the substitution of private preventative activities. In general, any move towards financing fire protection by more particularistic charges should improve allocative efficiency by providing incentives to balance different approaches to fire protection—e.g., the private provision of protective devices, the use of fireproof building methods, and so forth.

It is normally thought that the introduction of particular charges for police services would be unwise, since police protection is the epitome of the public good in local government. Nevertheless, the analysis in Chapter Seven suggests that a significant portion of services rendered by police departments are very private or particularized in their incidence; specific, easily identified individuals or groups reap most of the benefits. For example, in Connecticut cities it appears that a substantial portion of city police activity mainly benefits motorists as a group, many of whom live in jurisdictions other than the cities which now pay for these services through property taxes. This raises the issue of whether some of this outlay might not be better recovered by increased vehicle registration or parking fees instead of through the property tax. Rather similar arguments might be made about the specialized character of some property protection activities provided by local police departments. Again, as in the case of fire protection, if charges for police services were more closely aligned with costs of provision, the alternatives of insurance coverage or use of private security devices might be brought into better balance.

These analyses of the pricing and productivity characteristics of local public services again raise the issue of the tax relationships between different levels of government, particularly the deductibility of different local assessments against income taxes imposed by higher levels of government. Under current federal law, only local *taxes* are deductible as personal expenses in computing federal income tax liability. Changes in the law that would place user charges and property taxes on an equal footing in this regard would encourage user-charge financing and, hence, efficiency in service provision. As matters now stand, the income tax advantage discourages specific charges for local public services.

In sum, this analysis has been concerned with the many problems inherent in broadening the base of taxation and in improving the efficiency of service delivery in American cities, using the experiences of a few Connecticut cities, particularly New Haven, as in-depth case studies. How general are the findings of this analysis and how defensible are they? The discussion at several points highlights the limitations of a single case study of these complex phenomena. Nevertheless, certain broad policy generalizations do emerge. For example, it seems that the private sector might be employed to a greater extent in providing local public services, with a general gain in efficiency as a consequence. Certainly, more application of private sector market principles would be helpful: in particular, a closer alignment of charges for local public services with the specific costs of rendering these services. This is true whether the service is provided by private or public agencies. Presently existing federal income tax incentives do work against an improved alignment of the costs and charges for local public services and, hence, are perverse and undesirable from an efficiency standpoint. Efficiency considerations also argue for placing less reliance on one particular form of tax, the property tax, for meeting local fiscal needs. Like any form of very intensive and specialized excise taxation, the property tax can create perverse and counterproductive incentives.

In conclusion, some reforms can be identified in local financial practice, in tax policy, and in intergovernmental fiscal relations. None of these reforms would *dramatically* alter the fiscal position of older central cities such as New Haven. They would not reverse the underlying trends which have made suburban locations attractive for economic activity. However, by increasing the revenues of central cities and improving the efficiency of public service provision, they would help resolve the real dilemma caused by inadequate revenues and increasing demands for local services in central cities.

Notes

CHAPTER ONE

1. See, for example, Edgar M. Hoover, *An Introduction to Regional Economics*, New York: Alfred A. Knopf, 1971, especially Chapters 2 and 3.

2. William Alonso, *Location and Land Use*, Cambridge, Mass.: Harvard University Press, 1964.

3. Richard F. Muth, *Cities and Housing*, Chicago: University of Chicago Press, 1968, Chapters 1-3.

4. Some documentation of this impact in the period 1910-1920 appears in Leon Moses and Harold F. Williamson, "The Location of Economic Activity in Cities," *American Economic Review* (May 1967), 211-222.

5. Werner Z. Hirsch, *The Economics of State and Local Government*, New York: McGraw-Hill, 1970, Chapter 1.

6. D.F. Bradford, R.A. Malt, and W.E. Oates, "The Rising Cost of Local Public Services: Some Evidence and Reflections," *National Tax Journal* (June 1969): 185-202.

7. James W. Simmons, "Changing Residence in the City," *Geographical Review* (October 1968): 622-651.

8. Robert A. Leone, "Location of Manufacturing Activity in the New York Metropolitan Area," National Bureau of Economic Research, December 1971 (processed).

9. Charles M. Tiebout, "A Pure Theory of Local Expenditures," *Journal of Political Economy* (October 1956): 416-424. Jerome Rothenberg, "Local Decentralization and the Theory of Optimal Government," in *The Analysis of Public Output*, edited by Julius Margolis, New York: National Bureau of Economic Research, 1970: pp. 31-64.

10. John M. Quigley and Roger W. Schmenner, "Tax Exemption and Public Policy," *Public Policy* (Summer 1975): 259-298.

CHAPTER TWO

1. Benjamin Chinitz, "Contrasts in Agglomeration: New York and Pittsburgh," *American Economic Review, Papers and Proceedings*, (May 1961) Vol. VI, pp. 279-289.

2. Edward Louis Ullman, Michael F. Dacey, and Harold Brodsky, *Economic Base of American Cities*, Seattle: University Center for Urban and Regional Research, University of Washington Press, 1969, Monograph No. 1.

3. Edward Louis Ullman, Michael F. Dacey, and Harold Brodsky, *Economic Base of American Cities*, Seattle: University Center for Urban and Regional Research, University of Washington Press, 1969, p. 81.

CHAPTER THREE

1. 85% of all locally collected taxes were from the property tax in the 1969-70 fiscal year, according to the Bureau of the Census. See *Guide to Recurrent and Special Governmental Statistics*, Special Studies No. 62, Washington, D.C.: U.S. Government Printing Office, May 1972, Table 4, p. 16.

2. Specific figures for some U.S. cities in recent years are:

City	Year	% Exempt
Baltimore	1968	23.5
Boston	1967	47.2
Buffalo, N.Y.	1969	33.6
Denver	1968	19.7
New York City	1969	33.6
Pittsburgh	1967	32.4
Washington, D.C.	1969	52.3

Source: Alfred Balk, *The Free List*, New York: Russell Sage Foundation, 1971, p. 19.

3. See John Caffrey and Herbert H. Isaacs, *Estimating the Impact of a College or University on the Local Economy*, Washington, D.C.: American Council on Education, 1971.

4. See Alfred Balk, *op. cit.*

CHAPTER FOUR

1. Jewell Phillips, "Philadelphia's Income Tax After Twenty Years," *National Tax Journal* (Sept. 1958) Vol. 11, No. 3, pp. 241-253; John Lindsay, "Statement to the Legislature of the State of New York in Support of a Tax Program for New York City," March 9, 1966; and A.L. Warren, "Detroit's Experience," 28 *Academy of Political Science Proceedings* 30-32 (January 1968).

2. See State of Connecticut, *Information Relative to the Assessment and Collection of Taxes, 1971*, Hartford: State of Connecticut, 1972.

3. Kentucky Constitution Article 181; Kentucky Revised Statutes §91.260 (1969).

4. Much of this subsection's ideas derive from two very useful pieces by Peter

Mieszkowski. One is a review article, "Tax Incidence Theory: The Effects of Taxes on the Distribution of Income," *Journal of Economic Literature* (December 1969) 7: 1103-1124, and the other is "The Property Tax: An Excise or Profits Tax?" *Journal of Public Economics* (1972) 1: 73-76. Both articles cite much of the earlier relevant literature.

5. Peter Mieszkowski, "The Property Tax: An Excise or Profits Tax?" *op. cit.*

6. John M. Quigley and Roger W. Schmenner, "Property Tax Exemption and Public Policy," *Public Policy* 23 (3) (Summer 1975): 259-297.

7. Helen Ladd, "The Role of the Property Tax: A Reassessment," in Richard A. Musgrave (ed.), *Broad-Based Taxes: New Options and Sources*, (Johns Hopkins University Press: Baltimore, 1973).

8. See Roger Schmenner, "City Taxes and Industry Location," unpublished Ph.D. dissertation, Yale University, 1973.

9. For example, a prolonged strike at the Firestone Rubber Company pinched the city treasury in Akron. See L. Masotti and J. Kagelman, "The Municipal Income Tax as an Approach to the Urban Fiscal Crisis," *Journal of Urban Law* 45: 113 (1967).

10. John W. Cook, "Effects, Problems and Solutions of Central Collection of Municipal Income Taxes," *Case-Western Reserve Law Review* 19: 900-911 (1968).

11. In recognition of the expense incurred by an employer in withholding taxes, Missouri authorizes employers to retain 1½% of the tax they collect. *Mo. Stat. Ann.* §92.170 (1971).

12. A.L. Warren, "Detroit's Experience," *Academy of Political Science Proceedings* 28: 30-32 (January 1968).

13. U.S. Advisory Commission on Intergovernmental Relations, *State Constitutional and Statutory Restrictions on Local Taxing Powers.* Report A-14, Washington, D.C.: U.S. Government Printing Office, 1962. Future reference to this commission will be ACIR.

14. John F. Dillon, *Commentaries on the Law of Municipal Corporations* (5th ed.), Boston: Little, Brown, 1911, p. 235.

15. See, e.g., the following Connecticut decisions which held that "Municipalities have no powers of taxation other than that specifically given by statutes." *Chamberlain v. Bridgeport*, 88 Conn. 480, 91 A. 380 (1914); *Conn. Diesel Electric Corp. v. Stamford*, 156 Conn. 33. 238 A. 2d 410 (1968).

16. Virginia Code Ann. 58-80 (1969); 53 Pa. Stat. §15971 (Supp. 1975); 53 Pa. Stat. §6903 (1972). In 1972 Pennsylvania initiated a state income tax. 72 Pa. Stat. §730 et seq. (Supp. 1975). That statute, however, contained a savings clause which excepted local income taxes from the prohibitions of the Sterling and Tax Anything Acts. 53 Pa. Stat. §7359 (Supp. 1975).

17. *City & County of Denver v. Sweet*, 138 Colo. 41. 329 P. 2d 441 (1958); *Zielonka v. Carrel*, 99 Ohio St. 220, 124 N.E. 134 (1919); *Firestone v. Cambridge*, 113 Ohio St. 57, 148 N.E. 470 (1925); *Haefner v. Youngstown*, 147 Ohio St. 58, 68 N.E. 2d 64 (1946); *Cincinnati v. Cincinnati Oil Works Co.*, 123 Ohio St. 448, 175 N.E. 699 (1931); *Ohio Finance Co. v. Toledo*, 163 Ohio St. 81, 125 N.E. 2d 731 (1955). *Angell v. Toledo*, 153 Ohio St. 179, 91 N.E. 2d 250 (1950). When Ohio recently added a state income tax, the municipal income tax

was spared from preemption by a statutory savings clause. Ohio Code Ann. §5747.02 (Supp. 1974). A taxpayer action claiming that pre-emption is rooted in the state constitution and, therefore, not subject to legislative override was rebuffed by the courts. *Village of Ottawa Hills v. Joelson et. al.* (Ct. of Appeals, Lucas Cty.—4/4/75).

18. See, e.g., *Non-Resident Taxpayers Association v. Phila.*, 341 F. Supp. 1135 (D.N.J. 1971).

19. See, e.g., Edward G. Michaelian, "Comments (on Administration of the Municipal Income Tax)," *Academy of Political Science Proceedings* (January 1968) 28: 56-58. At that time Mr. Michaelian was the County Executive of Westchester County, New York—a suburban county contiguous to New York City.

20. 311 U.S. 435 (1940).

21. *Angell v. Toledo*, supra note 17; *Dooley v. Detroit*, 370 Mich. 194, 121 N.W. 2d 224 (1963); *Tax Review Bd. v. Belmont Labs*, 392 Pa. 473, 141 A.2d 234 (1958).

22. The percentage of individual income derived from unearned sources rises with the level of income. Joe Davis and Arthur J. Ransom, "An Evaluation of Municipal Income Taxation," 22 *Vanderbilt L. Rev.* 1321 (November 1969).

23. For example, Art. 8, Sec. 1 of the Pennsylvania Constitution states:

All Taxes shall be uniform, upon the same class of subjects, within the territorial limits of the authority levying the tax, and shall be levied and collected under general laws.

24. 157 U.S. 429 (1895).

25. *Murray v. Phila.*, 364 Pa. 157, 71 A.2d 280 (1950).

26. Id. at 170, 71 A.2d at 291. The statutory pre-emption rule referred to in the opinion was the Sterling Act.

27. Mich. Comp. Laws §141.619 (Supp. 1975) [prior permission of tax administrator now required]; N.Y. Gen. City Law §25-m sec. 4 (b) (2) (McKinney 1968).

28. Mo. Stat. Ann. §92.160 (1971); Ohio Code Ann. §718.02 (Supp. 1972).

29. Mich. Comp. Laws §141.615 (b) (1967).

30. See, e.g., 53 Pa. Stat. §6908(3) (1972); Del. Code Ann tit. 22 §902 (1974); Mich. Comp. Laws §141.503 (Supp. 1975), 141.611 (1967).

31. Jewell C. Phillips, "Philadelphia's Income Tax After Twenty Years," *National Tax Journal* (1958) 11: 241-253; Milton C. Taylor, "Local Income Taxes After 21 Years," *National Tax Journal* (1962) 15: 113.

32. See the Pennsylvania Constitution, supra n. 24.

33. N.Y. Gen. City Law 25-a sec. 3 (McKinney Supp. 194, 1968).

34. Del. Code Ann. tit. 22 901 et seq. (Supp. 1970). The rate structure was replaced by a 1½% flat rate, effective July 1, 1973.

35. *Betts v. Zeller*, 264 A.2d 290 (Del. Sup. Ct. 1970).

36. The first attempt by Philadelphia to levy a payroll tax was struck down

by the courts because the exemptions and credits provided therein violated the uniformity clause. *Butcher v. Phila.*, 333 Pa. 497, 6 A.2d 298 (1938).

37. See, e.g., Mich. Comp. Laws § 141.631 (Supp. 1975).

38. N.Y. Gen. City Law 25-a sec. 16 (McKinney 1968).

39. John W. Cook, "Effects, Problems and Solutions of Central Collection of Municipal Income Taxes," 19 *Case W. Res. L. Rev.* 900 (1968) at 902.

40. Id. at 904; Cleveland Ord. tit. 15, ch. 19 115.1901-02.

41. John W. Cook, *The Administration of the Earned Income Tax, in the Commonwealth of Pennsylvania*, pp. 14-17 (Harrisburg, 1964).

42. *Id.*, p. 15.

43. The legislation authorizing the creation of this district was struck down in *Four County Metro. Capital Improvement Dist. v. Bd. of County Comm'rs.*, 149 Colo. 284, 369 P.2d 67 (1967), because of a clash with Denver's Home Rule Powers. An extensive description of the proposed district appears in the text of the opinion.

44. 419 Colo, 284 at 287, 369 P.2d 67 at 70 (1967).

45. ACIR, *Local Non-Property Taxes and the Coordinating Role of the State.* 45 (A-9 1961) hereinafter cited as ACIR, A-9.

46. Md. Ann. Code, Art. 81, 283 (1975).

47. In 1968 the New Mexico legislature authorized a county surtax on the state income tax. *New Mex. Laws (S.S.) 1968, ch. 2.* Bernalillo County assessed a surtax of 43%. The levy was a "one-shot tax," Albuquerque Nat'l Bk. v. C.I.R. (N.M.) 82 N. Mex. 232, 478 P.2d 560 (1970), and apparently no subsequent authorization was ever passed.

48. ACIR, A-9 at 46.

49. Wis. Stat. Ann. § 71.14 (Supp. 1975). Similarly Ohio, in accordance with the provisions of Art. XII, § 9 of its state constitution, will return fifty per cent of the revenues collected from its newly enacted state income tax to local governments.

50. Ohio Const. Art. XII, § 9 (1955).

51. Alaska Stat. tit. 43 § 20.010 et seq. (1971); Neb. Rev. Stat. ch. 77, § 2714 et seq. (1971); R.I. Gen Laws tit. 44 § 30-1 et seq. (Supp. 1972); Vt. Stat. Ann. tit. 32 § 5811 et seq. (1970).

52. See, e.g., Neb. Rev. Stat. ch. 77 § 2714 which states in pertinent part:

Any term used in sections 77 § 2714 to 77 § 27124 shall have the same meaning as when used in a comparable context in the laws of the United States relating to federal income taxes, unless a different meaning is clearly required. Any reference to the laws of the United States shall mean the provisions of the Internal Revenue Code of 1954, and amendments thereto, . . . as the same may be or become effective, at any time or from time to time, for the taxable year. . . .

53. 239 Ark. 870, 394 S.W. 2d 731 (1965).

54. This view has prevailed in Nebraska, *Anderson v. Tiemann*, 182 Neb. 393, 155 N.W. 2d 322 (1967), the territory of Alaska, *Alaska Steamship Co. v.*

Mullaney, 180 F.2d 805 (9th Cir. 1950) and subsequently the state of Alaska, *Hickel et ux. v. Stephenson*, 416 P.2d 236 (Alaska 1966).

CHAPTER FIVE

1. American Public Works Association, *Refuse Collection Practices* (3rd ed.; Chicago: Public Administration Services, 1966), p. 271.

2. *Ibid.*, p. 244.

3. For a complete description of the data sources, see Peter Kemper and John M. Quigley, *The Economics of Refuse Collection*, Cambridge, Mass.: Ballinger Press, 1976.

4. J.E. Quon, M. Tanaka, and A. Charnes, "Refuse Quantities and Frequency of Service," *Journal of the Sanitary Engineering Division, Proceedings of the American Society of Civil Engineers* (April 1968): 403-420.

CHAPTER SIX

1. Expenditure information was compiled from municipal audit reports. Town Government Audit Reports are submitted annually to the State Finance Department. Expenditure data were collected from these reports.

2. "Municipal Fire Administration, 1967." Revised in 1974. See Public Technology, Inc., *New Provisions of the ISO Grading Schedule*, Washington, D.C., 1974. (Texas uses a different key rate system.)

CHAPTER SEVEN

1. Based on data from the U.S. Bureau of the Census. *Census of Governments*, 1957, Vol. 3, No. 5, "Compendium of Government Finances," and Vol. 2, No. 2, "Compendium of Public Employment," Washington, D.C.: U.S. Government Printing Office, 1973; and U.S. Law Enforcement Assistance Administration and U.S. Bureau of the Census, *Expenditure and Employment Data for the Criminal Justice System*: 1970-71, Washington, D.C.: U.S. Government Printing Office, 1973.

2. U.S. Department of Justice. Federal Bureau of Investigation, *Uniform Crime Reports for the United States, 1972*, Washington, D.C.: U.S. Government Printing Office, 1973, Table 2.

3. Paul A. Samuelson, "The Pure Theory of Public Expenditure," *Review of Economics and Statistics* (November 1954): 387-389.

4. Charles M. Tiebout, "The Pure Theory of Local Expenditures," *Journal of Political Economy* (October 1956): 416-424. See also James M. Buchanan, "An Economic Theory of Clubs," *Economica* (February 1965): 1-14.

5. For a discussion of spillovers and their effect on the provision of public services see Alan Williams, "The Optimal Provision of Public Goods in a System of Local Governments," *Journal of Political Economy* (February 1966): 18-33; William C. Brainard and Frank T. Dolbear, Jr., "The Possibility of Over-Supply of Public Goods: A Critical Note," *Journal of Political Economy* (February

1967): 86–90; and Mark D. Pauly, "Optimality Public Goods and Local Governments: A General Theoretical Analysis," *Journal of Political Economy* (May/June 1970) 78: 572–585.

6. In fact, Tiebout is unclear on this point; in some places he appears to assume there are no congestion externalities but at others he appears to assume they exist. For a discussion of this congestion problem, see William H. Oakland, "Congestion, Public Goods and Welfare," *Journal of Public Economics* (1972) 1:339–357; and Michael J. Boskin, "Local Government Tax and Product Competition and the Optimal Provision of Public Goods," *Journal of Political Economy* (January/February 1973) 81: 203–210.

7. For discussion of the importance of the fact that the choice of a community is also the choice of a location, see James M. Buchanan and Charles J. Goetz, "Efficiency Limits of Fiscal Mobility: An Assessment of the Tiebout Model," *Journal of Public Economics* (1972): 25–43.

8. The issue of where police service costs are incurred is an interesting one, although not central to an investigation of the desirability of special charges. Appendices B, C, and D deal directly with this issue. For another empirical study of the spatial distribution of police resources, see Charles S. Benson and Peter B. Lund, *Neighborhood Distribution of Local Public Services*, Berkeley: University of California, 1969.

9. The proportion of tax-exempt property in Bridgeport, 23.5% was obtained from the State of Connecticut, *Quadrennial Report of Real Estate Exempted from Taxation*, Hartford: State of Connecticut Public Document No. 52, March 1972.

About the Editors

John M. Meyer is a Professor at Harvard University and President of the National Bureau of Economic Research. He is the author of numerous books and articles and has participated in many government and public affairs activities.

John M. Quigley is Associate Professor of Economics at Yale University and Research Associate at the National Bureau of Economic Research. He is the co-author of *Housing Markets and Racial Discrimination* published by NBER in 1975 and *The Economics of Refuse Collection* published by Ballinger Publishing Company, Cambridge, in 1976. He has published papers in leading scholarly journals such as *The American Economic Review*, *The Journal of Political Economy*, and *The Quarterly Journal of Economics*.